FORERUNNERS: IDEAS FIR
MINNESOTA PRESS

Original e-works to spark

FORERUNNERS: IDEAS FIRST ...ak-
through digital works. Written between fresh ideas and finished books,
Forerunners draws on scholarly work initiated in notable blogs, social
media, conference plenaries, journal articles, and the synergy of aca-
demic exchange. This is gray literature publishing: where intense
thinking, change, and speculation take place in scholarship.

Carceral Humanitarianism

Carceral Humanitarianism
Logics of Refugee Detention

Kelly Oliver

University of Minnesota Press

MINNEAPOLIS

Published by the University of Minnesota Press
111 Third Avenue South, Suite 290
Minneapolis, MN 55401-2520
http://www.upress.umn.edu

The University of Minnesota is an equal-opportunity educator and employer.

Contents

Acknowledgments

Some sections of this book will appear in different forms in *Derrida Today Journal* (forthcoming); *Decolonizing Feminism: Transnational Feminism and Globalization,* ed. Margaret A. McLaren (London: Rowman and Littlefield International, forthcoming); *Critical Criminology Journal* (forthcoming); and *Logics of Genocide,* ed. Anne O'Bryne and Martin Shuster (Bloomington: Indiana University Press, forthcoming).

Introduction: From Political Right to Humanitarian Charity

DISCUSSING REFUGEES FROM NAZI GERMANY, Hannah Arendt ([1943] 1994, 110) says, "Apparently nobody wants to know that contemporary history has created a new kind of human beings— the kind that are put in concentration camps by their foes and in internment camps by their friends." Today, there may not be concentration camps, but thousands of refugees end up in detention centers, and hundreds of thousands are fenced into camps every year. Refugee camps and detention centers are an integral part of the so-called humanitarian response to the "refugee crisis." Often operating in extraterritorial and extra- or quasi-legal border spaces, refugee camps have become the answer to mass forced migration due to civil war, gang violence, famine, and drought. Far from the United Nations's (UN) post–World War II vision that persecuted peoples fleeing violence at home have a right to asylum and nonrefoulement, refugee camps and detention centers operate as check-points and management centers designed to ensure that refugees do not enter the host country rather than to ensure that they receive asylum, or even the basic human rights guaranteed by UN charters: clean water, food, and shelter, let alone security, freedom of movement, and dignity. In the words of sociologist Didier Fassin (2016), "whereas many European states once regarded asylum as a right, they now increasingly treat it as a favor. In parallel, the image of refugees had to be transformed, from victims of persecution entitled to international protection to undesirable persons suspected of taking advantage of a liberal system." What were considered political rights following the Second World War have been downgraded to humanitarian favors in the contemporary "refugee crisis."

Part of the problem is that even the United Nations High Commissioner for Refugees (UNHCR 1995a) defines the work of international law as humanitarian and not political: "beginning with the Statute of the Office, UNHCR's mandate has been described as a humanitarian one, meaning that actions in favour of refugees should be non-partisan and non-political with the sole concern being the safety and welfare of the refugees. This understanding of refugee protection as humanitarian work allows countries of asylum to respond to the needs of refugees without passing judgment on the country of origin, which is often a neighbouring state, while the acceptance of UNHCR as a humanitarian agency helps to ensure support for our work"; furthermore, the UNHCR incorporates human rights into humanitarian standards rather than political rights: "placing greater reliance on human rights standards as a basis for UNHCR's work does not jeopardize the humanitarian character of our activities, since international human rights law is itself non-political and non-partisan."[1] Here I attempt to show that humanitarian aid and human rights discourse are always political and partisan. Moreover, in terms of treatment of refugees today, humanitarian aid and human rights discourse have been coopted by military operations. Thus any claim to neutrality becomes suspect. Furthermore, tracing the history of humanitarianism demonstrates not only that it has never been neutral but also that it has its roots in war and violence. This is not to say that we should dispense with humanitarian aid and human

1. This module also outlines the various and complicated international conventions and treaties on human rights that affect refugees and asylum seekers.

rights; rather, we should critically consider how the uneasy alliance between humanitarian aid, human rights, and military operations produces refugees as either security risks or charity cases, that is to say, as criminals who deserve to be interrogated and incarcerated or as moochers who don't deserve anything but pity and a free handout.

Humanitarian aid organizations have become big business, often operating in tandem with state governments and the military. The process of applying for refugee status is difficult and fraught with problems, and most refugees end up living in squalid camps for decades before they are granted asylum, sent back home, or displaced into another temporary living situation. In terms of the multitude of international treaties and conventions governing humanitarian aid, human rights, and refugee treatment, refugee camps are not sanctioned by the UN. Indeed, many have come under attack for violations of basic human rights as outlined by UN charters (including refugees' rights to clean water, food, shelter, freedom of movement, security, dignity, and nonrefoulement or protection against return to the violence of their home countries). Although every refugee camp is different, most are overseen by a combination of government agencies, military personnel and police, and international humanitarian aid organizations, all ostensibly keeping borders of the host country secure from the so-called threats posed by refugees and providing refugees with the basic necessities to stay alive.

For those incarcerated or interned, detention centers and refugee camps are often places of abuse and always places of further trauma (Human Rights First 2009a; see also Granski, Keller, and Venters 2015). The irony is that people who have the courage to stand up to totalitarian governments, or fight for freedom, and flee persecution find themselves locked up or fenced in again in the name of the freedom and security of their hosts. Asylum seekers fleeing violence in their own countries meet another kind of violence in camps, and the freedom and security of refugees are sacrificed in the name of the freedom and security of "proper" citizens.

Even in countries proud of their democratic values, the value of an open society quickly closes itself off in the face of mass migration, as refugees and asylum seekers are managed, controlled, interrogated, detained, incarcerated, and interned in detention centers or refugee camps.

Carceral humanitarianism is today's response to the UN Refugee Convention originally designed to protect refugees from Nazi Germany. Carceral humanitarianism has replaced government resettlement policies created to address the situation of Jews and other displaced persons after World War II. With the newly formed UN Convention behind them, nation-states relatively quickly resettled people displaced during World War II. This is not the case today. Instead, today's refugees may spend a significant portion of their lives in refugee camps. Some of them grow up in refugee camps. Some of them die in refugee camps. While many of Arendt's insights into the status of stateless people still apply, refugees today are not so much stateless as border figures, who, rather than having their citizenship revoked by their home countries, are excluded by the host countries they seek to enter.[2] Not necessarily the *targets* of violence or persecution per se, many find themselves in the cross fire of civil war and must escape to save themselves and their families. Although the UN Refugee Convention and its amendments were designed to give

2. Wessel's (2015) analysis of the difference between Arendt's stateless person excluded from her home and today's refugee is provocative. On at least one point, however, we disagree. Wessel claims that Arendt describes a stateless person as someone whose citizenship is revoked and then is evicted from her home country. She bases much of her argument on the fact that today's refugees leave their homes voluntarily. The refugees Arendt describes in her most personal accounts also leave their homes "voluntarily" in the sense that, like today's refugees, they are escaping violence and murder. In fact, Arendt makes a point of problematizing this notion of "voluntary" and describing the prejudice of some in host countries who conclude that leaving voluntarily means giving up rights (see Arendt [1943] 1994). For another discussion of the difference between Arendt's refugee and today's refugee, see Rancière (2004).

the victims of political persecution the right to asylum, and legal remedies to procure protection, the status of today's refugees as victims of political persecution, and therefore as protected, is often ambiguous at best.

Furthermore, caught in the cross fire, many of today's refugees arriving in Europe are considered "collateral damage" in the so-called war on terror. The war on terror is fought without declarations of war or front lines. This is not a war between nation-states but rather comprises targeted attacks on pockets of power or subsets of populations (terrorists or dictators) in the name of security and democracy. The majority of people in these war zones are not terrorists, or even our enemies, yet they find themselves under attack, displaced, or fleeing for their lives. Caught in the cross fire of bloody civil wars fueled by covert post–Cold War politics, refugees from Iraq, Afghanistan, and Syria seek asylum in Europe, only to meet a chilly welcome at best and hostility and more violence at worst. The U.S. military and its allies use surgical strikes, drone warfare, and targeted assassinations to mitigate and control "collateral damage" in an age of "humanitarian warfare" where, in addition to delivering bombs and weapons, the military brings food and medical supplies and humanitarian aid organizations travel under military protection. More than ever, humanitarian aid and humanitarian warfare operate in tandem in an uneasy, but necessary, alliance between saving lives and killing—or letting die.

Massive refugee camps and detention centers attended by military forces, police, and humanitarian aid organizations are part of a system of population management. This carceral humanitarianism is the result of contemporary warfare as a way to control and manage populations and their movements. Carceral humanitarianism has become the norm in areas of conflict where refugees are suspected of being or becoming terrorists.[3] Rather than welcom-

---

3. For an insightful discussion of the figure of the refugee as terrorist, see Nail (2016).

ing refugees, their hosts assess the relative risks of taking them in versus turning them away. Individual refugees are assessed in terms of a risk–benefit analysis based on the threat or advantage they might bring to the host. The combination of sheer numbers and fear of terrorism leads to extended periods of detention for refugees, some of whom spend their entire childhoods in camps. Refugee camps the size of cities with only one or two water faucets, and lacking basic facilities such as bathrooms and medical care, have become squalid pits of despair for millions of people.

Contemporary detention centers and refugee camps are part and parcel of a system of carceral humanitarianism and "rescue politics" that turns refugees into criminals and charity cases simultaneously, which, in turn, becomes the troubling justification for "rescuing" them in order to lock them up or lock them in, increasingly in dangerous, disease-ridden, sorely inadequate conditions.[4] Refugees and asylum seekers become targets of a new humanitarian military. For example, in the case of Syrian refugees, navies and coast guards operating in the Mediterranean Sea patrol for boatloads of people risking their lives to flee violence at home. Their rescue at sea becomes a way of containing their unauthorized movement. Once rescued, migrants are sorted, contained within fences and checkpoints, and monitored. Their freedom of movement is severely limited, and they are often forced to live in deplorable conditions. As Martina Tazzioli (2015, 3) argues, migrants escaping wars and famine become "shipwrecked people" to be rescued in a problematic "rescue politics" that is as much about statistics as it is quality of life: "the government of migration is grounded on a politics of numbers that sorts people into 'risk' categories," where very few are eventually granted permanent asylum and allowed to legally enter the host country. With contem-

---

4. Tazzioli (2015) uses the phrase *rescue politics* and gives an insightful and engaged critique in "The Politics of Counting and the Scene of Rescue." For an implicit defense of rescue politics, see Wessel (2015). See also Tazzioli (2016).

porary rescue politics, the military approach that treats refugees like prisoners of war, terrorist threats, or criminals is fused with the humanitarian approach that treats refugees as charity cases to be rescued and saved. Military and humanitarian organizations operate in tandem, and often in coordinated efforts, both to save and to contain refugees.

Carceral humanitarianism is the outgrowth of humanitarian warfare in which war and aid are two sides of state sovereignty. International humanitarian aid and humanitarian warfare are bound together through a contradictory logic that simultaneously challenges and shores up state sovereignty. The fight for humanitarian space free from politics and national interests only highlights the intimate connections between humanitarian aid and national interests, which cannot be separated. Rather, nation-states rely on international humanitarian aid organizations to take care of mass forced migration and refugees, while their militaries police borders to capture, detain, and control the movement of those same people. In the name of human rights, and humanitarian concerns, state governments deploy military personnel to border regions (and so-called hotbeds of terrorism) to deliver both humanitarian aid and humanitarian warfare. Indeed, today's Western militaries, in the business of fighting terrorism, use humanitarian aid as much as they use smart bombs and drone strikes, both justified through increasingly complicated cost–benefit analyses and assessments of collateral damage.

In *Carceral Humanitarianism: Logics of Refugee Detention,* I deconstruct the opposition between humanitarian space and national sovereignty, and between humanitarian aid and humanitarian war, to diagnose a new form of humanitarianism, namely, *carceral humanitarianism*. Carceral humanitarianism has replaced any properly political solution to the "refugee crisis" by turning it into a matter of humanitarian aid or charity, on one hand, and of national security, on the other, thereby justifying military interventions. The protection of basic human rights of refugees supposedly ensured by international law is handed off to international humanitarian organizations or bartered among nation-states as bargaining chips in international trade agreements. In myriad increasingly complex ways, humanitarian aid operates in tandem with new forms of "humanitarian" warfare. The military and humanitarian aid organizations work together to deliver, manage, and police refugees' food, water, shelter, and medical care. We could even say that humanitarian aid is the flip side of humanitarian war.

Within the logic of humanitarian warfare, refugees become not only collateral damage but also fungible units to be exchanged between nations, where rich governments pay poorer ones to take in refugees so they won't have to. Furthermore, borders, border checkpoints, and border spaces have expanded to include *international* military and police forces, in order to catch, manage, interrogate, and contain refugees and asylum seekers before they even reach the shores of their host countries. Whereas borders are freely crossed by certain people, goods, and commerce, suggesting an open global economy, they remain closed to others, suggesting that borders are not just about territories and nation-states but also and moreover about policing certain groups of people. In the words of Julia Schulze Wessel (2015, 52), "whereas nation-state borders enclosed a specific territory and were institutions designed to regulate cross-border movements and transactions, today's borders enclose certain persons."

In an attempt to protect national security from those undesirables deemed threats, both humanitarian aid and humanitarian war operate according to the logic of collateral damage, wherein risks and benefits are calculated using computer algorithms designed to protect the host country while sacrificing the lowest number of civilian lives on both sides of the conflict. In this lesser-of-evils scenario, some will be sacrificed for the benefit of others. Yet, calculating collateral damage and the lesser of evils reduces human life—and all life—to exchange units whose value is calculated in terms of risks or benefits to the powers that be, namely, the United States, the European Union, and their allied military forces and governments. The relative value of human life, and all life, is calculated in terms that benefit certain people and make the lives of others disposable. At the extreme, and in its principles, the *logic* of collateral damage is a genocidal logic used to justify condemning some groups of people (or animals) and saving others. In the case of refugees, some groups of people are destined for camps and detention centers without basic resources, while a chosen few deemed beneficial to the host country and its economic well-being may be given proper paperwork to enter and work.

In *Carceral Humanitarianism,* I analyze the relationships between state sovereignty, humanitarian aid, humanitarian war, and rescue politics and conclude that although humanitarian aid may be necessary, and perhaps even desirable, it is not a properly political solution to a political problem.[5] Furthermore, I argue that even if we cannot, and should not, dismiss the importance of humanitarian aid, and the good work done by humanitarian aid organizations, we must critically analyze the current phase of humanitarian violence in relation to the history of humanitarianism, on one hand, and current military practices and discourses, on the other. Approaching contemporary humanitarian aid from various angles and different directions, I call into question the central role of international humanitarian aid organizations in addressing the refugee crisis, particularly insofar as those organizations are increasingly indebted to military operations and national agendas. The refugee crisis is not first a humanitarian crisis; rather, it is a political crisis caused by geopolitics on a global scale. And, unfortunately, today's carceral humanitarianism transforms mass forced migration into primarily a matter of national security, even as it incorporates discourses of human rights and rescue.

Human rights discourse and military rescue operations are not in themselves the problems. If that's all we've got, we need to use them. But the seemingly necessary alliance between war and aid, killing and protecting, interrogating and feeding, wound-

5. See Tazzioli (2015) for a brilliant overview of rescue politics.

ing and healing, and so on, inherent in the war on terror prevents any effective solution to the refugee crisis. Refugees have become pawns in the war on terror, sometimes seen as victims of terrorist organizations like ISIS and sometimes as terrorists themselves. Military strategy includes killing members of terrorist cells while providing food and aid to civilians at risk of radicalization to prevent the spread of terrorist ideology. Of course, the geopolitics of terrorism is complex, especially insofar as the United States has provided weapons and training for local insurgent groups that end up turning against the United States. And conflicts in the Middle East continue to play out Cold War politics with the United States and its allies, supporting one side, and Russia and its allies, supporting the other. Whatever the causes of the mass forced migration—Cold War politics, terrorist organizations, climate change and drought—the result is that millions of people are fleeing for their lives. And to spite current international policies supposedly ensuring the right to asylum, many refugees and migrants find themselves in precarious situations, risking death at sea or on dangerous journeys, only to arrive in squalid, makeshift camps on borderlands.

I begin this book by describing the scope of the problem: more than 60 million people have been forcibly displaced from their homes, more than 20 million of them are refugees seeking asylum, and another 10 million are defined as "stateless people" (UNHCR 2015a); furthermore, more than 20 million people live in camps and detention centers around the world (UNHCR 2015a; see also McKenzie and Swails 2015). The war on terror, civil war, gang violence, famine, and poverty caused by global warming are some of the reasons people are displaced both internally and outside their home countries. Yet protecting the sovereignty of some states and their national borders, and of certain people over others, has led to representations of refugees as either criminals or freeloaders, images used to justify detention, interrogation, population management, and control. Without state sovereignty and territorial borders, there wouldn't be refugee camps or detention centers.

Or put differently, if we embraced radical democratic values, and had open borders, the very distinction between citizen and refugee would disappear as people moved freely across borders. Fears about security (social, economic, religious, physical, cultural, etc.) produce the need for borders. These fears also produce perceptions of refugees as criminal, threatening, and abject. At best, refugees are seen as victims in need of rescue; at worst, they are seen as terrorist threats. In *Carceral Humanitarianism,* I deconstruct this opposition between rescue and security to show how humanitarian aid as rescue politics operates as the flip side of humanitarian war as security politics. I begin by showing how carceral humanitarianism and rescue politics do not satisfy the protection of refugee rights set out by the UN Refugee Convention. The squalid conditions in camps and lack of health care and freedom of movement in detention centers go against the UNHCR policy on basic human rights afforded to asylum seekers, whatever their status. If we take human rights as the standard, current policies toward refugees and asylum seekers fall woefully short.

Next, I argue that the UN requirements for refugee status put asylum seekers in an impossible subject position as both active agents fighting for their lives, on one hand, and helpless victims in need of rescue, on the other. In addition, practical considerations of translation and trauma make testimony to persecution problematic at best. The material difficulties to testifying to trauma in a system and language that are unfamiliar undermine the possibility of compelling testimony. To be granted refugee status, the UNHCR guidelines require that refugees fear for their lives, flee persecution, and escape violence in their home countries before they can even apply for refugee status. Refugees by definition, then, are traumatized by violence at home and during their escape, often making a perilous journey to a host country on whose shores they may arrive illegally. Though the UNHCR acknowledges a host of problems with interviewing refugees, these interviews too often become interrogations that put asylum seekers into the situation of reliving their trauma and the impossible situation of testifying both to their agency and to their lack of it in relation to their persecution. Continuing the line of reasoning from the first section, this section takes up some of the practical and theoretical problems of UN policies toward refugees in determining the right to asylum and protecting basic human rights.

The refugee crisis has been called a "humanitarian crisis" and a "crisis of human rights." In "Human Rights Discourse as Alibi for Humanitarian War," I briefly survey some of the philosophical and historical problems with the human rights discourse in relation to refugees. Starting with Hannah Arendt's critique of human rights as not only tied to citizen rights but also too abstract to protect stateless people, and continuing with Jacques Derrida's criticism of both categories of "human" and "rights," I argue that although human rights discourse may be useful, even necessary, in demanding basic resources for refugees, we cannot ignore the troubled history of human rights and how they continue to operate according to a logic of exclusion that necessarily leaves some abandoned and disposable. More importantly, I show how the human rights discourse is being used in the service of military operations and as an alibi for the collateral damage and lesser-of-evils utilitarian approach to the refugee crisis, which makes some lives more valuable than others and justifies treating some people as fungible commodities at best and as disposable "collateral damage" at worst.

Today, rather than addressing human rights per se, the approach to the refugee crisis by the United States and its allies, along with the European Union, is one of containing collateral damage and taking the lesser of evils. I continue my critique of the logic of calculability upon which policies of risk–benefit analysis are based, arguing that the utilitarian calculus used by both humanitarian aid organizations and humanitarian military operations reduces human life (and all life) to statistical calculations of risk or benefit to the organization or government doing the calculations. Even Doctors without Borders now uses complex risk–benefit computer modeling to set policies about where to send medical aid. This calculating machine at the heart of humanitarianism is dangerous, a so-called necessary evil. Yet, as Hannah Arendt ([1964] 2003, 36) reminds us, "those who choose the lesser evil forget very quickly that they chose evil."

Both humanitarian aid and humanitarian warfare operate according to logics of calculation. And in carceral humanitarianism, they usually operate together (if sometimes in an uneasy alliance) to deliver food, water, and medical supplies to regions of conflict and to protect aid workers while doing so. As part of the war on terror, and to reduce the risk of radicalization of people in war-torn areas associated with terrorists, the military itself delivers humanitarian aid. In "Humanitarian Warfare and Humanitarian Aid: Two Sides of the Same Sovereign," I argue not only that humanitarian warfare and humanitarian aid operate in tandem but also that nation-states create refugees and then pay humanitarian aid organizations to take care of them. National sovereignty is dependent on so-called neutral humanitarian space, which occupies an ambiguous space on the outskirts and borders of host countries. This neutral humanitarian space, often guarded by state police and military, is far from independent of state sovereignty. To the contrary, humanitarian space is coopted to maintain national sovereignty against the threat of migrants, asylum seekers, and refugees. In other words, within carceral humanitarianism, refugees operate as both a threat to national sovereignty and the justification for shoring up borders.

In the remainder of *Carceral Humanitarianism*, I continue to deconstruct the notion of humanitarian space by demonstrating that humanitarian aid organizations are not only dependent on state governments but also, and moreover, part and parcel of the logic of state sovereignty. Following Derrida, I trace the Christian roots of that sovereignty back to the sacrifice of Christ on the cross, which is closely associated with the history of humanitarian organizations, most especially the very first international humanitarian organization, the Red Cross. Relying on historian Michael Barnett's history of humanitarian aid organizations, I challenge the notion of neutral humanitarian space, not only because aid organizations have always been closely connected to the military and government support, but also because they have always delivered ideology along with bandages. From the civilizing mission of Christianity to the mission of globalization, humanitarian aid organizations are not immune from politics. Yet, as long as governments rely on humanitarian aid organizations to manage refugee populations, they have an alibi for not providing what Arendt, and contemporary philosophers such as David Owen, demand, namely, a political solution (rather than a humanitarian solution) to a political problem.[6] As my analysis attempts to show, however, humanitarian aid cannot be separated from politics. It has always been political. On one hand, there is no neutral humanitarian space, and the calls for such neutrality point to its impossibility. On the other hand, using humanitarian aid as an alibi allows nation-states to postpone a "properly political" solution to mass forced migration.

If contemporary logics of proportionality employed by both humanitarian aid organizations and humanitarian military operations are designed to mitigate and control violence and death to avoid the worst violence and death, according to calculations of the lesser of evils, then we must ask, what is the most evil, or the worst evil? Usually, we think of genocide as the worst evil, and the "worst" is often shorthand for the "final solution" and the Holocaust. Since the end of World War II, and the Cold War, the "worst" has become associated with the possibility of nuclear war, even the destruction of the entire planet. Following Derrida, I rethink that worst as a result of the logic of calculation taken to the extreme at the expense of all other worldviews. When lives

6. For insightful contributions to debates over the political status of refugees, see the work of David Owen (2014; 2016a; 2016b; 2016c). Although I am in agreement with much of Owen's analysis, using a deconstructive methodology, I take a very different approach. Owen does an excellent job defending a radical version of human rights and the need for political solutions to the so-called refugee crisis.

become fungible and exchangeable, we risk the "worst." In this regard, insofar as contemporary humanitarian warfare operates according to the logic of utilitarian calculations of collateral damage that make some lives disposable, it risks the "worst."

In "A New Form of Genocide," I argue that the conditions in most refugee camps and detention centers and the political construction of the group identity "refugee," combined with policies of collateral damage and lesser-of-evils scenarios, meet the definition of genocide set out by the UN. Most particularly, policies that treat refugees as collateral damage or units of exchange, where some lives are more valuable than others as calculated through risk–benefit analysis, renders the lives of refugees fungible and therefore ultimately disposable. The fact that the United States and the European Union pay other countries to keep refugees from crossing their borders makes clear that the lives of these people can be bought and sold like so much cargo to be held in port or lost at sea. The UN definition of genocide goes beyond mass murder to include any group whose members are denied basic human rights on the basis of their membership in that group. I argue that refugees constitute such a group. Whether they are treated as charity cases or security threats, insofar as the basic needs of refugees are managed by humanitarian aid organizations rather than by governments, and insofar as governments manage asylum seekers primarily as security threats rather than refugees, their treatment leads to the cordoning off of a group of people who are often given substandard subsistence, fenced in or detained, and implicitly condemned to "slow death."

In sum, humanitarian aid is both the cure and the poison. It's the cure insofar as right now it is the only chance we have for helping refugees under the current immigration and asylum policies of most nation-states. That is to say, until we move beyond nation-states and their alibi of humanitarian aid, groups such as Doctors without Borders and the Red Cross are absolutely necessary, and their volunteers and aid workers are praiseworthy. Yet, as long as we hold on to the alibi of humanitarian aid, a more properly political solution will not be forthcoming. As long as we continue to turn asylum seekers into criminals and charity cases, in need of incarceration or rescue, then we will have no hope of addressing the fundamental crisis of mass migration due to terrorism, civil wars, drought, famine, and climate change. As long as we continue to treat refugees as fungible or disposable, we risk the "worst."

"Rescue Politics"

WHEN WE CONSIDER REFUGEES TODAY, the statistics are overwhelming. It is difficult to fathom the depths of this "humanitarian crisis" that leaves millions fleeing for their lives. Using statistics and eyewitness reports, I set the stage by briefly touching on the global proportions, and dismal living conditions, of refugees today. Although the numbers are staggering, my argument is based not on numbers, nor on utilitarian calculations, when considering forced migration and asylum seekers but rather on the ethical and political stakes of discourses of rights and responsibilities where refugees are concerned. I start by sketching the scope of the political problem posed by carceral humanitarianism in terms of people affected worldwide, people subjected to violence at home, perilous journeys to escape, dangerous border spaces, and inadequate basic resources in refugee camps. Even if they make it to "safety," they are often subjected to appalling conditions at best and more violence at the hands of their hosts at worst. The subsequent sketch is merely an outline of the problem to set the stage for my analysis of the relationship between humanitarian aid and humanitarian war that follows.

Last year, global forced displacement reached an all-time high, with at least 65.3 million people (at a rate of 24 people every minute) displaced from their homes by conflict and persecution (Edwards 2016). Of the entire world's population, 1 in every 113 people is a refugee or asylum seeker, and of those, roughly half are women and girls, with 51 percent younger than eighteen years of age (Edwards 2016). In 2015, more than a million people fled to Europe seeking asylum, primarily from Syria, Afghanistan, and Iraq. The vast majority of them arrived by sea, making a perilous journey that has cost thousands their lives. At least thirty-seven hundred people died crossing the Mediterranean Sea in 2015. And given that thousands more go missing or are unaccounted for, it is impossible to determine how many people have actually died (BBC News 2016). Because many refugees and asylum seekers are forced to attempt illegal border crossings, until their dead bodies wash ashore, many are not counted in statistics of the missing or dead (see Tazzioli 2015). Statistics of perilous crossings and deaths coming in for 2016 are significantly higher than for other years.[1] For example, in just the first six weeks of 2016, crossings increased tenfold, and so did deaths (*Al Jazeera* 2016). Of the refugees escaping from Syria, at least 1 million women were of childbearing age, and at least seventy thousand of them were pregnant when they fled (United Nations Population Fund for Arab States 2016). Their children born in refugee camps are stateless, not just because their mothers' fled their countries of origin but also and moreover because most Middle Eastern countries base citizenship on soil rather than on birth, whereas most host countries base citizenship on birth rather than on soil (or do not recognize refugees). This means that an entire generation of Syrian refugees will be without papers, will be stateless people (Spencer 2016). The director of the United Nations Population Fund says, "We are dealing with a lost generation of children who have not gone to school, who are not

1. The UNHCR reports that in the first eight months of 2015, more than three hundred thousand refugees and migrants crossed the Mediterranean Sea seeking asylum in Europe. More than twenty-five hundred died in those months, and in 2014, thirty-five hundred died. See Fleming (2015). Also see Tazzioli (2015) for a discussion of the unaccounted-for dead.

registered, who are stateless" (Spencer 2016). Last year, the majority of refugees were under eighteen years old. By the end of 2014, the number of people assisted by UNHCR had reached a record high of 46.7 million (UNHCR 2015a).

Still, there is another "humanitarian crisis" that doesn't get the media attention of refugees fleeing to Europe. In Africa, there are more than 3 million refugees, 12.5 million internally displaced people, and another 700,000 stateless people (Momodu 2015). The UNHCR reports that "of the estimated 529,000 maternal deaths that occur globally every year, 48% are in Africa. And, refugee women and newborns are particularly vulnerable. For each maternal death, at least 30 more suffer from infection, injury and short or long term disability" (UNHCR, n.d.). As with women and girl refugees everywhere, African women refugees are at very high risk of sexual violence, first in areas of civil conflict, then on the road to escape, then in refugee camps and outside camps when searching for firewood and from the authorities within the camps. "According to Amnesty International, individuals who commit rape and other violence against women and girls often enjoy near total impunity. Some of the barriers to justice for these crimes include: inability of victims to identify their attackers; lack of will by authorities to investigate; threats and intimidation techniques to prevent victims from testifying; weaknesses in the legal framework; and the use of traditional customs of conflict resolution that do not discourage perpetrators from negative behavior" (Miller 2011, 78).

These statistics are mind-boggling. More astounding is that most refugees end up living in camps for decades before resettlement. Unlike refugees from World War II, who were resettled by 1952, many of today's refugees spend decades in a permanent state of temporary living. For example, the largest refugee camp in the world, Kenya's Dadaab, is twenty-five years old; it was built for 90,000 refugees but now holds more than 420,000. On average, a refugee lives twelve years in a camp (McClelland 2014). Furthermore, conditions in most refugee camps are dangerous and unhealthy; people are forced to live in overcrowded, makeshift tent compounds without adequate basic necessities like bathrooms, clothing, and food. For example, in Dunkirk camp in France, more than three thousand refugees live in rat-infested tents pitched in ankle-deep mud and human waste with only two water faucets; one resident says, "This place is for animals, not for human beings" (Sputnik International 2016).

Unfortunately, Dunkirk is not an isolated example. Calais, another camp in France near the Channel Tunnel, was known as the "Jungle" and housed more than six thousand at its peak, most living in squalor, where "sanitation ranges from appalling to nonexistent" and "human shit litters every 'path' of the camp" (Charlton 2015). The residents call it the Jungle because they're treated like animals (see Charlton 2015). Echoing many others, one resident told a reporter, "We are humans, not animals" (Gentleman 2015). Violent protests and clashes with police throwing tear-gas resulted from the French government bulldozing a large section of the camp in March 2016, further displacing already displaced people (see Courbet 2016). At least 129 children have gone missing since the camp was razed (see *RT News* 2016).

Recently, the Greek interior minister, Panagiotis Kouroublis, called the Idomeni camp on Greece's border with Macedonia "a modern-day Dachau, a result of the logic of closed borders" (Worley and Dearden 2016). "Despite being planned for just 2,500 people, the camp hosts around 12,000 refugees—many from Syria and Iraq—in wet, cold and muddy conditions" (Worley and Dearden 2016), which Red Cross officials warn are rife for the spread of disease. These are the refugees who "feel like we are dying slowly." And now, because the route to Greece from Syria has been effectively closed, refugees flee through Libya, making an even more dangerous crossing of the Mediterranean Sea into Italy—one that recently led to more than one thousand people dying and another four thousand being rescued in a matter of days, in what a spokesperson for Save the Children called "a massacre" (Yardley and Pianigiani 2016).

Thousands of miles away in the United States (which has been slow to take in Syrian refugees), refugees live in detention centers that look like and are run like prisons, with locked cells and "inmates" wearing jumpsuits, and where processing refugees takes months to years (Cone 2015).[2] The United States operates the world's largest immigration detention system, and most centers provide substandard health care (see Janet 2016). As in other prisons, conditions in detention centers are often poor, with inadequate health care, lack of facilities and personnel, and preventable deaths, including suicide (Granski, Keller, and Venters 2015). A recent investigation into subpar health care in detention centers confirmed that the lack of health care contributed to several deaths: "system-wide problems remain, including a failure to prevent or fix substandard medical care that literally kills people," and isolation is improperly used to confine people suffering from mental health issues (Human Rights Watch 2016).

Human Rights First (2009b) reports that in the United States, "since 2002, the number of immigrants detained each year has more than doubled—with an increase from 202,000 in 2002 to an estimated population of over 440,000 in 2009. The average daily-detained population has grown from 20,662 in 2002 to 33,400 in 2009. As this network has grown, problems of poor conditions, inadequate medical care, difficulty accessing legal counsel, or receiving religious services have also worsened. Of the hundreds of thousands of immigrants annually who find themselves caught up in this system—all for civil immigration violations—a few thousand are asylum seekers, individuals who come here to ask for protection from persecution." In addition, many of these immigrants and asylum seekers have been denied due process and are locked up without legal recourse. According to Human Rights Watch (2016), "most of the hundreds of thousands of people held in this system each year are subject to harsh mandatory detention laws, which do not allow for an individualized review of the decision to detain

2. See Devon (2015). Thanks to Jennifer Newman for bringing this to my attention.

them during their immigration proceedings." Many asylum seekers suffer in detention centers for months, some for years, before their cases are resolved.

Although Syrian refugees arriving in Europe get the most media attention, there is another American refugee crisis taking place outside the spotlight, one involving primarily women and children fleeing Central America for Mexico and the United States. Tens of thousands of women and children are fleeing violence in El Salvador, Honduras, Guatemala, and parts of Mexico. Worldwide, El Salvador, Honduras, and Guatemala rank first, third, and seventh, respectively, for rates of homicides of women (see UNHCR 2015b). The UNHCR reports "a nearly fivefold increase in asylum-seekers arriving to the United States from the Northern Triangle region of El Salvador, Guatemala, and Honduras" and a "thirteen-fold increase in the number of requests for asylum from within Central America and Mexico—a staggering indicator of the surging violence shaking the region." Most of the refugees are women escaping repeated rape, assault, extortion, threat from armed criminal gangs, watching their children being recruited into gangs or killed, and watching other family members being murdered or disappeared, while authorities do nothing. Often, they reach a breaking point when their lives are in imminent danger unless they flee immediately. But escaping presents its own dangers, as women are forced to pay exorbitant fees to "coyotes" and then suffer more rape, beating, and sometimes murder by these human traffickers (see UNHCR 2015b). If they reach Mexico or the United States, these women face detention, a lack of adequate health care, and lengthy interrogations, which too often exacerbate their psychological trauma; and then, there is no guarantee that they will be given asylum rather than sent back home to face more violence.[3]

3. UNHCR (2015b, 47) reports that "some [women] felt detention exacerbated traumas suffered at home and in flight. As Alexa from El Salvador put it: 'They should help facilitate the asylum process so that one doesn't suffer in detention centers. They shouldn't be causing more harm.'

Deputy High Commissioner L. Craig Johnstone stated in 2008 that "refugee women are more affected by violence against women than any other women's population group in the world" (Dobbs 2008). The Refugee Council (2009, 4) reports that "all refugee women are at risk of rape or other forms of sexual violence." Yet, the number of women refugees affected by sexual and gender-based violence is impossible to access for several reasons, among which are that refugee women are escaping war zones without facilities for addressing rape, many refugee women do not report sexual assault or gender-based violence, and some refugee women are shunned for admitting sexual assault or gender-based violence.[4] Many refugee women come from countries where the shame associated with rape is even greater than it is in the United States and where repercussions for reporting may be grave. The Refugee Council's "Vulnerable Women" report concludes, "Some women, including many of those claiming asylum on the basis of gender-specific persecution, come from countries where sexual violence by security forces has been institutionalized. Women coming from conflict zones will be especially affected: 'war rape' has reached epidemic proportions. . . . Rape has been used strategically, as a weapon of war in attempts to destroy the opposing culture" (4).

Women refugees fleeing violence at home are at a far greater risk than men of encountering violence, especially sexual assault

---

One Mexican woman described experiencing severe anxiety each time the officers closed and locked the doors to her cell. She said, 'It is better to be free and to die by a bullet than to suffer and die slowly in a cage.' . . . Women interviewed for this report emphasized that the experience of being detained remains with them far beyond release. 'The things I lived through in detention have marked me for life,' said a Salvadoran woman who recently was granted asylum. 'Please remember that we are human beings. I didn't want to come here, but for me it was a question of life and death.'"

4. For a more sustained treatment of women refugees, see Oliver (forthcoming). See also Baillot, Cowan, and Munro (2009) and Ferris (2007).

and rape, en route to their host countries and while in refugee camps. They risk assault at the hands of human traffickers, smugglers who insist on sex in exchange for help or food, fellow refugees, and even police and soldiers along the way or guarding the camps. In general, the journey to safety is perilous for men and women, but women and girls face unique challenges both on the road and in the camps. Inadequate food and medical care disproportionately affect women, especially pregnant women, who lack access to prenatal care, adequate nutrition, and midwives or hospital facilities. In addition, a lack of feminine hygiene products, birth control, and OB-GYN services presents unique problems for girls and women. Furthermore, insofar as women are seen as primarily responsible for children, their burden on the road and in camps is wrenching. And because of their close connection with children, often the effects of disease and death among their children take a physical and psychological toll on women that goes unaddressed in overcrowded refugee camps lacking food and water, basic medical supplies and medical personnel, and adequate shelter.

We could go so far as to say that the dismal circumstances of most refugees—men, women, and children—whether in U.S. detention centers or international refugee camps, meet the criteria for genocide set out by the UN, which includes debilitating living conditions: "less obvious methods of destruction, such as the deliberate deprivation of resources needed for the group's physical survival and which are available to the rest of the population, such as clean water, food and medical services; Creation of circumstances that could lead to a slow death, such as lack of proper housing, clothing and hygiene or excessive work or physical exertion" (United Nations 2014). Hundreds of thousands of people are forced to live in situations without adequate clean water, food, shelter, and medical care; and even if they do get those basic needs met, it is often at the expense of their personal security, liberty, mental health, and dignity.

Indeed, no matter how many mind-boggling statistics we accumulate, we can never approach the human element of the equation, which cannot be quantified or reduced to a mere number. Furthermore, statistics piled one on top of the other can lead to "disaster fatigue," even for those most committed to helping. Perhaps this is why most news stories begin and end with "human interest" angles that focus on the experiences of particular individuals (mostly children, like the tragic poster boy for the refugee crisis, the washed-up body of tiny, three-year-old Aylan Kurdi, or the small, ash-covered face of Omran Daqneesh as he was placed in an ambulance in Aleppo) to make the numbers come to life. Many news reports on the refugee crisis in Europe or Africa refer to a "humanitarian crisis" and the lack of human rights or humane living conditions. But the rhetoric of humanity cuts both ways. For example, one aid worker in the Calais camp described the situation: "There's no official structure, no camp leadership, just a group of people surviving, a random collection of humanity camped in a field" (Gentleman 2015); the same report goes on to say that "some of the newer British volunteers are cheerful as they hand out supplies. 'It's touching, isn't it?' they say, brightly. 'The humanity is amazing!'" (Gentleman 2015). Simultaneously, as we've seen, many of the refugees call on their hosts to treat them like human beings instead of animals. The list of horrors from camps and detention centers goes on and on. And so do the statistics on numbers of displaced and dead, to the point that it becomes impossible to fathom fully the depths of the current "humanitarian crisis."

The UN Refugee Convention defines a refugee as a person who, "owing to well-founded fear of being persecuted for reasons of race, religion, nationality, membership of a particular social group or political opinion, is outside the country of his nationality and is unable or, owing to such fear, is unwilling to avail himself of the protection of that country; or who, not having a nationality and being outside the country of his former habitual residence as a result of such events, is unable or, owing to such fear, is unwilling to return to it" (United Nations General Assembly 1951). Many refugees today who are fleeing war and violence, or drought and famine, in their home countries do not meet the letter of this definition insofar as they are not being persecuted for reasons of race, religion, nationality, or membership in a particular social or political group. In fact, the largest group of refugees (those escaping violence in Syria) are not technically refugees according to this definition. The women fleeing violence in Central America have been considered a protected group only relatively recently in the United States but not in all countries. And even in the United States, women must demonstrate that they are being persecuted because of their group identity or political opinions, which is often difficult to prove.

Although the UN insists that seeking asylum is a lawfully protected act, in practice, it is difficult to do so legally with all of the documentation required, including passports issued by home countries; in turn, illegal entry authorizes the host country to detain and interrogate asylum seekers. Indeed, the rights granted to asylum seekers by international law are very similar to rights granted to criminals, with the significant exception of lack of due process or access to legal counsel. For example, in the United States, in the name of Homeland Security, and security against terrorist threats across the globe, in actuality, regardless of international law, asylum seekers have very few rights. They can be detained indefinitely without counsel.

The fact that *refugee status* in particular requires the applicant to make it to a host country and then prove his persecution at home means that those fleeing war and famine must have a means of escape (which costs money), make it out of their home countries, make an illegal border crossing (unless they have proper passports and visas, which are extremely difficult, if not impossible, to obtain in regions fraught with war and violence), and then prove persecution (which is also difficult for those fleeing war or famine). This leads to "rescue politics," where boatloads and truckloads of refugees risk their lives and are either rescued or perish. This also means that they must find their own way out of a precarious and dangerous situation and face further trauma and violence, only to arrive (if they are lucky) in a host country that accepts them into a camp or detention center where they are further traumatized, even interrogated as criminals or terrorists. If and when they reach a host country, and are sorted, managed, detained, and fenced into camps, they become members of a group defined by law as "refugees" or "asylum seekers," who are too often denied basic human rights as defined by the UN (clean water, food, shelter, health care, freedom of movement, security, and dignity), if not also persecuted and then allowed slowly to perish. If they don't die from violence or starvation at home, or on the perilous escape, they face disease, and what some refugees call "slow death," in the camps.

Impossible Testimony

EVEN THE WORDS *refugee* and *asylum* connote criminality. The *Oxford English Dictionary* defines a *refugee* as "one who, owing to religious persecution or political troubles, seeks refuge in a foreign country: a. Originally applied to the French Huguenots who came to England in 1685 after the revocation of the Edict of Nantes. b. A *runaway fugitive from justice*" (emphasis added). And *asylum* is defined first as "a sanctuary or inviolable place of refuge and *protection for criminals and debtors* from which they cannot be removed without sacrilege" and second as "a benevolent institution affording shelter and support to some class of the afflicted, the unfortunate, the destitute, e.g. '*a lunatic asylum*'" (emphasis added). From the beginning, then, refugees have been seen as criminals, debtors, and mentally ill. Although the words have evolved, their associations have not. The figure of the "refugee" is still considered destitute, criminal, and mentally ill. Insofar as she must leave her home country, she becomes homeless and dependent on others for basic needs; insofar as national and international law requires that she leave her home country and make her request for asylum on foreign soil, and usually do so as an illegal alien, she is made criminal; and the trauma she has suffered at home, the trauma that justifies and legitimates her status as refugee and asylum seeker, creates her as mentally ill. For, to legitimately gain refugee status and be accepted into her host country, she must convincingly testify to the *trauma* of violence and *fear* of persecution. She must convince authorities that she is afraid for her life; that she has been traumatized; in effect, that she has suffered mentally as well as physically.

And yet, as the UNHCR guidelines for interviewing asylum seekers make clear, cultural differences and translation problems are significant dangers in the determination of refugee status. The guidelines give a striking example of the danger of mistranslation: "A Turkish asylum-seeker, applying for refugee status in Switzerland, stated that he had escaped arrest by hiding in the mountains near his home town. The application was rejected. Among the reasons given was the fact that the town was situated amid hills. For the Swiss interviewer there were no mountains in the region and thus the applicant was considered to be not credible. However, in Turkish, the term 'mountain' also applies to hilly regions." As the guidelines warn, "notions of time, of truth and falsehood can also vary from culture to culture and give rise to misunderstandings that put the asylum-seekers' credibility in doubt" (UNHCR 1995b). And yet, despite the monumental risk of misinterpretation and mistranslation, every day, interviews determine the fate of asylum seekers based on this faulty process.

The difficulties of testifying to trauma are compounded when the trauma involves sexual assault, because many women are extremely reluctant to talk about rape. In the United States, where there is marked improvement in "blame the victim" standards and shame over being sexually assaulted, rates of reporting rape continue to be shockingly low; and when women do report, their testimony continues to be dismissed or ignored. Most women report feeling ashamed or being shamed, even further traumatized, by the process of reporting.[1] In cultures where "blame the victim" is the norm, and women face ostracism and retribution for report-

---

1. I discuss sexual assault and rape in the United States and U.S. rape culture in Oliver (2016b).

ing rape, rates of reporting sexual assault are even lower, there are fewer resources for reporting, and the negative consequences of reporting are greater.[2] Refugee women have the added difficulty that they are on the move, away from whatever social or institutional support systems they may have had at home, which makes reporting sexual assault even more difficult in purely logistical terms. To whom do they report? And when they do, the perpetrator is rarely found or prosecuted. In some cases, police, border guards, aid workers, so-called peacekeepers, and community leaders—the very people who are supposed to be helping them—have sexually exploited refugee women (Ferris 2007).

Furthermore, asylum seekers formally testifying to sexual violence and assault at hearings often encounter what some legal scholars call "a tendency amongst some asylum professionals to marginalise, trivialise or ignore accounts of rape; a tendency that, we argue, both occludes the narratives of asylum-seeking women who have suffered sexual violence, and poses substantial obstacles to securing justice" (Baillot, Cowan, and Munro 2013, 1). In an earlier study, these researchers concluded that refugee women face even more difficulties than other women when reporting sexual assault and even poorer treatment by legal professionals in the criminal justice system (Baillot, Cowan, and Munro 2009). Refugee women are not able to "tell the story" in their own words because most interviews are conducted through interpreters, whose very presence adds yet another witness in

2. In her short overview and literature review, Liz Miller (2011) discusses various studies that indicate that sexual violence is a fact of life for refugee women and that reporting rates are very low. In addition, when rapes are reported, authorities rarely find or prosecute the perpetrators: "the most difficult element of 'rape culture' for advocates to overcome within refugee populations is the cultural perception of rape. First of all, sexual violence is a difficult and painful topic for victims to discuss because sex is a taboo topic, and to report rape feels like an invasion of privacy. Moreover, in many communities the act is seen as an embarrassment to the community and the victim's family" (78; see also Baillot, Cowan, and Munro 2013).

front of whom refugee women who are victims of sexual assault must testify.

The UNHCR guidelines on interviewing asylum seekers include several sections on addressing and navigating trauma to determine the truth of the applicant's testimony and point out that people suffering from trauma may give inconsistent testimony, be unable to testify, or even become aggressive when questioned as a result of trauma. Refugee women traumatized by sexual violence are least likely to be "heard" and believed (Baillot, Cowan, and Munro 2013). The guidelines also insist that interviewers verify the truth of the testimony and resolve inconsistencies through confrontation techniques. While the UNHCR convention clearly states that an asylum seeker must fear returning to her country, and must fear persecution based on belonging to a certain group in particular, in this case, women, the interview guidelines admit that fear may adversely affect the interview process. The guidelines specially address sexual violence, indicating, "In the context of seeking asylum, the female victim of sexual violence may be hesitant or unable to speak about such events. Moreover, a female victim of sexual violence may be shunned by her family and alienated from members of her community. The interviewer will therefore have to use a variety of gender-sensitive techniques to obtain information from women during the interview process" (UNHCR 1995b). These techniques include providing all female interviewers and interpreters and, in extreme cases, allowing written instead of oral testimony. As several studies make clear, however, these guidelines are not necessarily, or even usually, followed (e.g., see Baillot, Cowan, and Munro 2013; Miller 2011).

Even if the guidelines were followed to the letter, testimony to trauma, especially sexual trauma, is vexed, particularly in the context of asylum seekers, and even more so when the legitimacy of their claims to asylum rest on claims of trauma resulting from sexual violence. In general, we might ask, how does she testify to fear in a way that is convincing? The guidelines warn against rehearsed, scripted testimony and against retraumatizing applicants.

So how does an interviewer determine the veracity of claims to fear? How can fear be quantified and accessed? Assuming that fear is an emotional or mental state, what formula can interviewers use to assess the legitimacy of fear insofar as it corresponds to actual events? Indeed, within trauma theory and psychoanalytic theory, trauma is often considered an experience that cannot be put into words, an experience that falls outside of linear time and rational comprehension. Furthermore, what does it mean to testify to the trauma of persecution? And what does it mean to *prove* trauma, especially the mental or psychological trauma of sexual violence? Finally, how much trauma is enough to justify asylum, and how does a person convince administrators and interviewers that his trauma is real?

Although humanitarian aid organizations, including Doctors without Borders, now include mental health professionals and psychologists, there are woefully inadequate resources to treat mental health issues in refugee camps and migrant detention centers, even though many refugees and asylum seekers fleeing war and violence suffer from posttraumatic stress disorder. One study of refugee camps in Germany "found that half of refugees are experiencing psychological distress and mental illness resulting from trauma" and "one fifth of refugee children are also suffering from PTSD" (Finnerty 2015). As historian Michael Barnett suggests, we have entered an era of trauma where the violence of persecution at home is measured not only in terms of physical scars but also in terms of mental scars and where humanitarian aid includes treatment not only for physical wounds but also for mental wounds.

We could go further and claim that current international policies and practices governing the treatment and status of refugees require testimony to trauma that puts the refugee into an impossible subject position with regard to her own experience.[3]

3. For a sustained discussion of the paradox of testifying to your own trauma and oppression, see Oliver (2001).

Refugees are required both to prove suffering and trauma in their home countries and also to demonstrate that they did everything in their power to overcome those obstacles before fleeing. This is to say, they must testify to both their helplessness and their own resilience in escape. They must prove both their radical victimization and their own sovereignty. Diana Tietjens Meyers (2016) calls these the two victim paradigms: the pathetic victim and the heroic victim.[4] Implicitly, current policies require both positions at once. Being accepted as a legitimate refugee requires documentable and verifiable fear and trauma. Yet, this position as "shipwrecked" person to be saved or rescued undermines agency and self-sovereignty and creates an aporetic subject position impossible to maintain. Asylum seekers are expected to take matters into their own hands, to actively flee violence, but in doing so, they become helpless, passive victims to be rescued—victims of rescue politics.

Speaking for herself and other refugees from World War II before the United Nations had established the rights of asylum for refugees, Hannah Arendt ([1943] 1994, 114) says, "If we are saved we feel humiliated, and if we are helped we feel degraded." She points out that because refugees "voluntarily" entered detention centers and camps, their interment is justified (115). Despite UN policy and international law that guarantee the right to asylum, this sentiment is alive and well today, as some callously claim that if refugees don't like conditions in the camps, they can stay or go back home. Yet, in what sense is the perilous journey of most refugees "voluntary"? The status of the refugee calls into question categories of active and passive, sovereign and victim, voluntary and forced. Arendt argues that refugees are considered both pariahs

---

4. Meyers (2016) calls for an alternative approach to victims' testimonies that does not reduce them to pathetic or heroic victims but rather considers human rights abuses within a political framework in which criteria are set out for what counts as an abuse. Her analysis powerfully demonstrates that victim testimonies can make a difference and that human rights discourse can be effective in transforming both policies and realities.

sucking up resources that could go to rightful citizens and parvenus, social climbers not truly fleeing violence or trauma but rather migrating for a better life abroad. Many of Arendt's observations are still apt today when reactions to images of refugees fleeing violence in Syria include both fear of them taking jobs or resources from host countries already dealing with high unemployment and poverty (such as Greece and Turkey) and bewilderment as to why they have cell phones and nice clothes if they're so bad off. And whether seen as charity case or social climber, Arendt says, "history has forced the status of outlaws upon both, upon pariahs and parvenus alike" (119). Today, rescue politics and carceral humanitarianism produce the helpless, homeless refugees as charity cases and criminals to justify detaining, monitoring, controlling, and containing them.

Humanitarian Warfare and Humanitarian Aid: Two Sides of the Same Sovereign

JUST AFTER THE TERRORIST ATTACKS OF 9/11, Derrida warned, "An earthquake has completely transformed the landscape in which the ideal of tolerance took its first form" (Borradori 2003, 126). The "humanitarian crisis" resulting from the influx of refugees in Europe is part of the fallout of this earthquake. Or, using current military parlance for assessing what we can and cannot tolerate, refugees have become "collateral damage" in the war on terror. Indeed, the utilitarian calculus of collateral damage is at the epicenter of this changing landscape. As he so often does, Derrida points out that the ideal of tolerance has its roots in religion, specifically Christian charity. And, like other concepts we inherit from Christianity, including forgiveness, hospitality, witnessing, and abolitionism, tolerance is inherently linked with sovereignty. "Tolerance," Derrida says, "is always on the side of the 'reason of the strongest,' where 'might is right'; it is a supplementary mark of sovereignty, *the good face of sovereignty,* which says to the other from its elevated position, I am letting you be, you are not insufferable, I am leaving you a place in my home, but do not forget that this is my home" (Borradori 2003, 127, emphasis added).

When it comes to refugees, humanitarian aid is this "good face" of state sovereignty. Confident in our tolerance, humanitarian aid eases our conscience, despite the tremors shaking the foundations of any notion of "just war." For the war on terror is a war without clearly defined territories, nation-states, enemies, front lines, national or international law, or even traditional declarations of war. Today, when covert rules of engagement loosely agreed upon in secret meetings between lawyers, politicians, and military commanders have replaced both national and international law, contemporary Western warfare sits on two extranational, extraterritorial pillars: on one side, international military forces, and on the other, international humanitarian aid organizations, the two frequently working together to create more "humane warfare." In terms of refugees, this translates into the unhappy choice of treating those fleeing violence as either threats to be contained in detention centers or charity cases to be saved in camps, where the difference between the carceral model and the rescue model is ever more difficult to discern. Barbed wire fences and checkpoints surround refugee camps, and military personnel deliver medical and food supplies to the very people they've just bombed. Surgical strikes, smart bombs, and targeted drone warfare are circumscribed by a chain of command of lawyers operating according to extrajudicial powers, yet strictly adhering to international "rules of engagement" based on complex computer calculations of collateral damage using some classified utilitarian calculus purportedly designed to transform the war machine into a humanitarian machine, reducing death to a minimum and saving as many (human) lives as possible, all without leaving the military or the government vulnerable to media or legal scandal.

Yet, this seemingly extrajudicial warfare is all about the law, not only appeasing government and military lawyers who fear lawsuits but also and moreover laws of probability and proportionality through which the force of law becomes justified using statistical cost–benefit analysis. The calculating machine creates the humanitarian war machine, and the computer becomes an alibi for targeted killing both to limit and to justify collateral damage. *Because* it is extranational and extrajudicial, more than ever, Western warfare rationalizes its tactics with rules of engagement so that commanders in the CIA and MI-6 who make the rules, if not those actually sitting in tin cans in the middle of the Nevada desert who pull the triggers, can sleep at night. And, if this cool, calculated distance war isn't enough to ward off ethical insomnia, today's military delivers clean water, food, and medical supplies along with air-to-surface missiles and grenades. Walls, fences, and checkpoints, seemingly proof of homeland security, are actually evidence of the threat to this security, a threat that justifies more force in this might-makes-right brand of humanitarian tolerance and humanitarian warfare.[1]

International humanitarian aid and international high-tech military forces operate as two sides of the same sovereign, made stronger by threats to it. International humanitarian space and international military forces simultaneously call into question national sovereignty and shore it up. These two pillars, humanitarian aid and humanitarian war, operate according to an autoimmune logic by which the greatest threat to their survival is also what sustains them, namely, bloody wars, terror attacks, and human suffering. War creates refugees, and then we wage more war to address the situation of refugees, as in Syria, where the European Union and its allies have agreed to "work to improve humanitarian conditions inside Syria" (now supposedly with help from Turkey) (European Commission 2016), where improving humanitarian conditions includes continued military assaults on ISIS. The practical interdependence between military operations and humanitarian operations, especially in war zones, has been well documented, particularly by historians Michael Barnett and Eyal Weizman.[2] These scholars, among others, demonstrate how globalized international aid in so-called neutral humanitarian space,

---

1. For an extended analysis of walls, fences, and checkpoints as evidence of the failure of state sovereignty, see Brown (2014). For a discussion of "the wall" between Palestine and Israel, see Weizman (2007).

2. For documentation of the close relationship between the military and humanitarian aid, see Neuman and Weissman (2016), Weiss (2013), Barnett (2013), and Weizman (2011).

defined as beyond national borders and beyond politics, remains dependent on government agencies for funding and physical space and on military forces to protect and deliver aid workers and supplies.

A deconstructive analysis of the notion of "humanitarian" reveals the conceptual dependence of humanitarian aid on state sovereignty by tracing the concept of "humanitarian" back to its Christian roots and the ultimate sovereignty of God. In addition, deconstruction calls into question ethics and politics based on the notion of the *human,* the centerpiece of both humanitarian aid and human rights discourses, even when these discourses are at odds with each other, as they frequently are in debates over whether aid organizations should take sides or take up political causes. Deconstructive analysis asks us to consider, in the words of Derrida, "new claims for what are called *human* rights, [and thus] through *the earthquakes* of this century, the seisms at the frontier that displace even the definition of the front and the frontier, [in] the wars without war" (Derrida 2009b, 119, emphasis added). Whereas others have shown that humanitarianism remains in the service of state interests in terms of practical politics, I attempt a deconstructive analysis of the relationship between humanitarian aid (or space) and state sovereignty. To put it bluntly, state sovereignty creates the legal category "refugee," which necessitates humanitarian aid organizations to step in to literally fill the space between state borders, and between citizens and refugees, which in turn fuels the police and military response to shore up borders and state sovereignty. This circular logic of sovereignty turns like Robinson Crusoe's wheel, which becomes a metaphor for autoimmunity in Derrida's 2001–3 seminars, *The Beast and the Sovereign.*

Arguably, the history of the concept of autoimmunity in Derrida's thinking is a sort of reclamation of the term from biology back to politics, where it originated. In other words, biologists imported from politics, and not vice versa. Some accuse Derrida of "getting it wrong," insofar as he talks about autoimmunity (which, according to biologists, is the immune system attacking the cells and organs of its own body) as if it were immune deficiency (which is the immune system not protecting the body against foreign bodies coming from outside).[3] As some scholars have pointed out, however, these metaphors of aliens, foreign bodies, invasion, and immunity originated in political discourse and were subsequently imported into biological discourse (e.g., see Miller 2011; Naas 2009).

In his first uses of the metaphor of autoimmunity, Derrida relates *immunity* to *community,* and the concept of autoimmunity eventually becomes associated with the necessary impulse of democratic communities both to open themselves to foreigners, on one hand, and to protect themselves from foreigners, on the other (e.g., see Miller 2011; Naas 2009; Haddad 2013). In even more stark terms, we could say, the autoimmune impulse is the impulse of democracy to protect itself from the nondemocratic actors and policies that threaten it by applying nondemocratic actors and policies itself: in the name of democracy, we shut down democratic processes. Ultimately, for Derrida, autoimmunity is the democratic body not only turning against itself but also protecting itself, "its chance and its fragility."[4] Democracy is necessarily autoimmune in that

   3. Ezster Timár (2016) has recently argued, "What is crucial for Derrida here is the apparent contradiction that for saving a life we have to disarm the apparatus whose function is to save the same life by protecting it from external threat. In other words, autoimmunity here, is NOT identified in the way medical science discusses autoimmunity, that is, as a process in which an overly active immune system attacks the cells belonging to the organism it protects as its own, but rather as its very opposite . . . immunology justifies this reversibility" (see also Timár 2015; Timár 2014).
   4. Derrida (2005, 46) claims, "Democracy is the only system, the only constitutional paradigm, in which, in principle, one has or assumes the right to criticize everything publicly, including the idea of democracy, its concept, its history, and its name. Including the idea of the constitutional paradigm and the absolute authority of law. It is thus the only paradigm that is universalizable, whence its chance and its fragility." He also says, "Democracy has always wanted by turns and at the same time two incompatible things: it has wanted, on the one hand, to welcome only men, and on the condition that they be citizens, brothers, and compeers [*semblables*], excluding all

it must open itself to foreign others and yet must also protect itself from others who threaten it. This autoimmune logic points to the tension between ethics and politics, between the unconditional and the conditional, between the pure and the contaminated, and even between theory and practice, insofar as these poles are in necessary tension with each other. Autoimmunity opens up the possibility of community, hospitality, and democracy, even as it necessitates the self-contradictory impulse to protect by destroying (Naas 2009). Derrida (2003, 124) is concerned with the "aporia between the positive and salutary role played by state sovereignty and citizenship as a form of protection, and on the other hand, the negative or limiting effects of state sovereignty when it closes its borders to noncitizens or monopolizes violence. Once again the state is both self-protecting and self-destroying, at once remedy and poison. The *pharmakon* is another name, an old name, for this autoimmunitary logic."

Following Derrida, I use this figure of autoimmunity as a metaphor for the contradictory impulse both to protect and to destroy the social and political body in the name of democracy, hospitality, or, more to my point, humanity and humanitarianism. Discussing the development of the concept of autoimmunity in his work, Derrida says, "I tried to formalize the general law of this autoimmune process in 'Faith and Knowledge,' a text that initially grew out of a conversation about forgiveness and went on to speak about a 'democracy to come' in relation to the secret, forgiveness, and unconditionality in general, as a concept that exceeds the juridico-political sphere and yet, from the inside and the outside, *is* bound up with it. The formalization of this autoimmune law was there carried out around the *community* as *auto-eo-immu-nity* (the common of community having in common the same duty or charge

the others, in particular bad citizens, rogues, noncitizens, and all sorts of unlike and unrecognizable others, and, on the other hand, at the same time or by turns, it has wanted to open itself up, to offer hospitality, to all those excluded" (34; cf. 63).

[*munus*] as the immune), as well as the auto-co-immunity of humanity and particularly the *autoimmune humanitarian*" (Derrida 2005, 20, emphasis added). So, too, as we will see, contemporary humanitarian warfare is bound up with contemporary humanitarian aid in an autoimmune relationship that takes us back to the Christian roots of sovereignty.

The Christian Roots of
State Sovereignty

HUMANITARIAN AID ORGANIZATIONS and humanitarian military operations share not only resources but also a history that takes us back to Enlightenment notions of the *human* and *humanity* out of which humanitarianism was born. As we know, the question of Enlightenment humanism, or what is proper to man, as defined against the machine, the animal, and God, is never far from Derrida's analysis of questions of responsibility—particularly, the secret, the witness, hospitality, perjury and pardon or forgiveness, and the death penalty. From the time of his lectures on theology and politics of the mid-1980s to the ten seminars titled *Questions of Responsibility* given from 1991 to 2001, Derrida continually and repeatedly returns politics and philosophy back to their theological—specifically Christian—roots, which ultimately lead back to the sovereignty of God, mirrored by the self-sovereignty of man created in his image. In his final seminar, *The Beast and the Sovereign,* Derrida continues with the theme of the theological (particularly Christian) foundations of sovereignty.

Taking a quick survey of how Derrida relates humanist discourses of tolerance, forgiveness, and hospitality to sovereignty, particularly Christian notions of God's sovereignty, gives us a blueprint for considering humanitarianism as the flip side of this same tolerant–intolerant sovereignty. For example, in the late 1990s, discussing the South African Truth and Reconciliation Committee, and other political contexts, where forgiveness made its way into political discourse as a way of addressing "crimes against humanity," Derrida (2001, 31) says, "If . . . the crime against humanity is a crime against what is most sacred in the living, and thus already against the divine in man . . . then the 'globalisation' of forgiveness resembles an immense scene of confession in progress, thus a virtually Christian convulsion-conversion-confession, a process of Christianisation which has no more need for the Christian church." Derrida finds this Christian stain in the Hegelian notion of forgiveness as reconciliation, redemption, and salvation and its secular uptake in contemporary political discourse, insofar as it reinscribes forgiveness within an economy of exchange that ultimately takes us back to Christ's sacrifice on the cross as payment for human sin, on one hand, and the absolute sovereignty of God to grant forgiveness, on the other.

Likewise, in his lectures on hospitality, Derrida reveals how the Enlightenment ideal of hospitality we inherit from Kant is indebted to its religious heritage, even as Kant limits hospitality to the right of visitation in the context of commerce (for Kant, the need for commerce having given rise to political or public rights in the first place). The Kantian cosmopolitan right to hospitality is one of Derrida's favorite examples of conditional hospitality, which always necessarily operates in tension with unconditional hospitality. The tension between conditional and unconditional is apparent in Pauline hospitality, which explicitly links hospitality to citizenship when St. Paul says, "You are no longer foreigners abroad, you are fellow-citizens of the Saints, you belong to the House of God" (Derrida 2001, 20; Ephesians 2:19–20). Yet, as Derrida insists, "there is no hospitable house. There is no house without doors and windows. But as soon as there are a door and windows, it means that someone has the key to them and consequently controls the conditions of hospitality. There must be a threshold. But if there is a threshold, there is no longer hospitality" (14). The House of God, then, above all signals the mastery or sovereignty of the ultimate host and the key to salvation.

As Derrida points out, *host* has its roots in the Latin *hostis* (which means not only "host" but also "guest," "visitor," "stranger," or "foreigner") and in the Latin *hospes* (a compound of *hostis* and *potis*, which means "lord and master of the house"). Thus the concept of hospitality we inherit from this Christian tradition contains within it the sovereign mastery of one's own house, family, country, and nation, which signals a "self-limitation or self-contradiction in the law of hospitality" that Derrida associates with what he comes to call *autoimmune logic* (5, 14).[1] Once again, the ultimate host is the Holy Host, welcoming us into the House of God through the transubstantiation of Christ's body and blood on the cross.

The contradictions of Christianity and its autoimmune logic come to the fore in Derrida's analysis of the death penalty, particularly insofar as the sanctity of human life is used to justify both capital punishment and its abolition. The whole bloody history of enlightened executions (along with their abolition) is indebted to Christian humanitarianism, nailed to the thorny issue of the crucifixion of Christ's human body. Again talking about the theological roots of modern politics, in the first session of the *Death Penalty* seminars, Derrida (2013, 2) announces that the seminar will be about "the religion of the death penalty" and "the death penalty

---

1. It is noteworthy that in several places in his discussion of hospitality, Derrida suggests that women are sacrificed for the sake of hospitality between men. For example, for better or worse, he ends one lecture with a reference to the biblical story of Lot offering his virgin daughter in exchange for peace among the tribes of Israel. Derrida suggests that our contemporary notion of hospitality is heir to this tradition that sacrifices women, particularly offering them up for rape (Derrida and Dufourmantelle 2000, 153–55). This suggestion might seem extreme, except for the media and government's reluctance to address reportedly hundreds of sexual assaults in Cologne, Germany, on New Year's Eve 2016 by groups of migrant men against German women for fear of appearing racist or antirefugee. Of course, it is controversial whether gangs of Arab men attacked women, as initially reported in mainstream and right-wing media. For example, see Shams (2016). For the right-wing media, see the *Local* (2016).

as religion." In session 8, he identifies an eighteenth-century "humanitarian" transformation of the death penalty with the invention of the "humanitarian machine," the guillotine, by a former Jesuit of the Society of Jesus, Doctor Guillotin, who justified his invention as a more humane capital punishment, a supposedly painless, instantaneous death offering no more than a "breeze" on the back of the neck (193–95).[2] Additionally, the humanitarian machine offered an anonymous killing, rendering the executor no more than a machine operator, a mere cog in the wheel of the killing machine. The same humanizing logic is at work in drone warfare, where thousands of miles separate the executioner from the condemned, and offers the illusion not only of instantaneous death, and anonymous killing, but also of humanitarian concern for limited loss of life or controlled collateral damage.[3]

In the nineteenth century, Derrida finds Christian humanitarianism at work not only in defense of a more humane death penalty but also in the abolitionist discourse taking place at the same time, particularly that of Victor Hugo, who promises that the "gentle law of Christ will finally permeate the legal code" and that crime will be considered an illness. Then hospitals will replace prisons, doctors will replace judges, and the cross will replace the gallows, signaling the substitution of Christ's blood for that of the sinner. It's not just Dr. Guillotin, then, who turns punishment into medical science; the abolitionist Hugo proposes Christic "balm and unction" as a curative. On both sides, as Derrida concludes, "the medicalization of justice is done in the figure, history, and narrative of Christ" (208). As we will see, with humanitarian aid, the balm and unction of Christ become both cure and poison, operating according to the autoimmune logic of Christian charity based on the violence of the cross; after all, Christianity, like Western

2. For a discussion of the fantasy of instant death, see Oliver (2013; 2016a).

3. For a discussion of drone warfare in terms of Derrida's *Death Penalty* seminars, see Wills (2014).

philosophy, begins with the death penalty. This autoimmune Christianity, embodied in the figure of the crucified Jesus, both man and God, human and divine, moral and immortal, suffering and saved, leads to the humanitarian attempt to solve the contradiction by focusing on Christ's embodiment and suffering, that is to say, what makes him like us. And now we are getting to the crux of the matter, namely, how the history of the concept of "humanitarian," which engenders contemporary notions of humanitarian aid and humanitarian space, is nailed to the cross through identification with the human suffering of Jesus.

A Brief History of Humanitarianism

EARLY HUMANITARIANISM was indebted to Kantian humanism, including not only his ideals of human dignity and Kingdom of ends, and his cosmopolitan notion of rights accorded to human beings qua human above and beyond national citizenship, but also his humanitarian view of Christ. The very first uses of the word *humanitarian* in the late eighteenth century referred to those who believed Christ's nature was human only and not divine, with Kant leading the way.[1] One of the earliest encyclopedia entries on "humanitarian" begins, "The Humanitarian or Unitarian Christology makes Christ a mere man, though the wisest and best of men, and a model for imitation. . . . Kant may be said to have inaugurated the modern Humanitarian view. He regarded Christ as the representative of the moral ideal, but made a distinction between the ideal Christ and the historical Jesus" (Herzog and Schaff 2011, 58). Indeed, in *Religion within the Limits of Mere Reason,* Kant says, "For let the nature of this human being well-pleasing to God be thought as human, inasmuch as he is afflicted by just the same needs and hence also the same sufferings, by just the same natural inclinations and hence also the same temptations to transgression, as we are" (Kant 1999, 6:64).

1. As in B. Hobhouse's reply to Rev. Randolph Let in 1792, "some Humanitarians would tell you that the doctrine of the atonement is perfectly compatible with the simple humanity of Christ" (*OED Online*).

In the aftermath of what is considered to be the first truly international natural disaster, the 1755 earthquakes in Lisbon, Kant wrote three essays explaining how the earthquakes were a natural phenomenon and not punishments from God and how, in the face of the inhospitality of nature, we must come together as a cosmopolitan community. Even foreshadowing the notion of humanitarian political neutrality and humanitarian space, Kant suggests that a noble prince would stop warring on a country that was the victim of a natural disaster like an earthquake (Kant 2015, 1:461). In his second essay, titled "History and Natural Description of the Most Noteworthy Occurrences of the Earthquake That Struck a Large Part of the Earth at the End of the Year 1755," Kant claims, "Whatever damage the . . . earthquakes [may] have . . . occasioned [*erweckt*] men on the one side, it can easily make it up with profit on the other side," and he mentions natural hot springs as a benefit: "We know that the warm baths, which in the process of time may perhaps have been serviceable to a considerable part of mankind for promoting health, owe their mineral property and heat to the very same causes from which happen in the bowels of the earth [and] the inflammations that shake it" (Kant 2015, 1:456). On the cosmic balance sheet, Kant's firm belief in Providence assures him that the benefits of earthquakes outweigh the costs. In this sense, Enlightenment humanitarianism begins with a Christian teleological version of cost–benefit analysis.

The use of *humanitarian* in relation to Christ's human suffering continues into the twentieth century. But, in the mid-nineteenth century, the word *humanitarian* takes on its modern meaning of having concern for humanity (although even then, it was originally used as a derogatory term to describe those who were overly sentimental). At the same time, *humanitarian* became associated with widespread human suffering, a meaning in use today in phrases such as "humanitarian crisis" or "humanitarian catastrophe." *Humanitarianism,* then, in all of its uses, is related to suffering, and originally to Christ's suffering on the cross. On one hand, the concept "humanitarian" originates with the bloody and violent sacrifice of Jesus, and on the other, it signals his salvation through the sovereign power of God, who welcomes all sinners into his house through Christ's blood.

We don't need the *Oxford English Dictionary* or archival research to know that in practice, humanitarian aid has been, and in many cases continues to be, essentially linked to Christian charity, especially in the context of war. The oldest and largest humanitarian aid organization, the International Committee of the Red Cross, still uses a symbol from medieval Christianity signifying Christ's blood on the cross. And in its beginnings, along with bandages and medicine, nurses delivered a Christian civilizing mission. The relation of justice to the balm and unction of Christ is at work in the birth of humanitarian aid, beginning with the founding of the International Committee of the Red Cross in 1863 in Geneva, Switzerland, around the same time that Hugo was arguing for abolitionism from his exile off the coast of Normandy. From the start, however, the Red Cross had its detractors. For example, nurse Florence Nightingale told its founder, "Such a society would take upon itself duties which ought to be performed by the government of each country and so would relieve them of responsibilities which really belong to them . . . and render war more easy" (Greenspan 2013). And by World War I, "the American Red Cross was considered so essential to the war effort . . . that a Wisconsin public official was convicted under the Espionage Act for calling it, among other things, 'nothing but a bunch of grafters'" (Greenspan 2013).

Contemporary Humanitarian Space

TODAY, humanitarian aid organizations have complicated relationships with both the military and national governments, upon which many rely for protections, access, and funding. As Florence Nightingale predicted, the military and government rely on humanitarian organizations to take over where they leave off. Governments create humanitarian crises, and then aid organizations, under the watchful eye of state governments and their militaries, step in to manage them. National borders and humanitarian space operate as two sides of state sovereignty, propping each other up through a tense, often oppositional relationship. Challenges to state sovereignty continue to grow, whether from groups like ISIS and the Taliban, groups that operate beyond state sovereignty or in semisovereign states like Syria, on one hand, or from refugee crises and forced migration, on the other. So, too, challenges to humanitarian sovereignty from governments, militaries, and humanitarian organizations themselves have led to demands for independent humanitarian space, apart from any nation or political cause. On one side, we have state governments creating the very refugees that challenge their sovereignty, and on the other side, we have humanitarian aid organizations reproducing the force of law and carceral logics of state sovereignty within refugee camps. All the while, both nation-states and humanitarian spaces demand protection of their sovereign borders. Refugee camps, which have become semipermanent cities, supposedly operate independently of any national government and are cordoned off by walls, fences, and checkpoints. While humanitarian spaces are looking more like internment camps, the military is in the business of delivering humanitarian aid, and both operate in the service of humanitarian warfare based on the calculus of costs and benefits.

Historian Michael Barnett has identified three ages of humanitarianism: first, the civilizing Christian mission to uplift the fallen, particularly on the battlefields of Europe, by working independently yet in tandem with government forces; second, after World War II, aid agencies focused on a related mission of bringing development to the Third World to address an expanding conception of humanity and the forces of globalization, while struggling to carve out a neutral humanitarian space apart from politics. But, as Barnett (2013, 31) concludes, "it would prove painfully difficult to do, especially because aid agencies were increasingly dependent on states and international organizations for their funding. . . . In places like Biafra, Vietnam, Cambodia, and Ethiopia, aid agencies discovered that they were part of the war and pawns for combatants, struggling to figure out how close to get to politics without getting burned and how to deliver aid without unwittingly prolonging conflict or suffering."

If the first phase of humanitarian aid is marked by politics posing as blind faith in the Christian civilizing mission, the post-Holocaust second phase is an eye-opening challenge to the naive assumption that the entire world wants an injection of Western democratic humanism along with its penicillin. The first humanitarians joined forces with the colonizing missions of the West, whereas the second phase involved the painful process of decolonialization played out by proxy in the Cold War, which left humanitarian groups wondering whose side they were on—and how it was possible to avoid taking sides in the first place.

Following World War II, as Allied governments divided up Axis territory, the struggle between the civilizing mission and the right to self-determination was playing out, not only in the former colonies, but also in the birth of the UN Charter signed by fifty countries in 1945, the Universal Declaration of Human Rights ratified in 1948, and the Refugee Convention adopted six years later, in 1951. For example, immediately following the war, Western countries argued that the rules of extraterritoriality giving diplomatic immunity applied only to "semi-civilized countries" like China and Japan and not to "civilized nations" "whose sovereign rights," in the words of literary historian Lydia Liu (2014, 391), "would not admit of such exceptionality as extraterritoriality without undermining the very idea of sovereignty." At the same time, original drafts of the charter and universal declarations gave European nationals "special privileges in non-European settings so that European life, liberty, dignity, and property would be protected" (391).

The conflict between the Christian civilizing mission and universal human rights came to light in debates over the original UN Charter, especially when some signatories from European nations proposed excluding "uncivilized" and "non-self-governing" colonies from those granted human rights (Liu 2014, 389). Looking back at those debates, the irony is, as Liu puts it, that "Western democracies, mainly colonial powers, embraced cultural relativism, but it was rejected by the overwhelming majority of Third World nations who were staunch advocates of universalism" (396). The Declaration of Universal Human Rights, in the name of which international peacekeeping forces deploy military troops and humanitarian aid to bring Western humanitarian values to the rest of the globe, was actually imported. As Liu's analysis shows, Western universal human rights as they operate in international law today were, in a significant sense, we might say, "made in China." In other words, in its infancy, the Western actors involved in formulating the Universal Declaration of Human Rights exhibited the autoimmune logic Derrida associates with antidemocratic policies and practices, such as Homeland Security surveillance and the restriction of personal freedoms levied in the name of democracy—in the case of Homeland Security, limiting personal freedom and limiting universal human rights are carried out in the name of national sovereignty and citizen protection.

Tensions between state sovereignty and international law, human rights and self-determination, and relativism and universality were evident not only in the terms of the first UN debates but also in the performance of the debate, which took place, and continues to take place, in multiple languages in which *human* and *rights* mean different things, if they exist at all. Originally, the official languages of the UN were English and French, but soon were added Russian, Chinese, Arabic, and Spanish. And today, the Universal Declaration of Human Rights has been translated into 389 languages (Liu 2014, 413). We could add problems of testimony and translation, singularity and repeatability, to this thorny nest in which contemporary human rights were born.

Barnett's third and present phase of humanitarianism, dominated by human rights discourse, operates in uneasy tension with continued demands for apolitical humanitarian space and is as much about international security or protection as it is about medicine and food (Barnett 2013, 31). Humanitarian organizations have entered the business—and big business it is—of addressing the dangers of "failed states" in a global economy by targeting the causes of the collapse of state sovereignty, including poverty and civil war, the supposed breeding grounds for terrorism.[1] The war on terror has put humanitarian aid at the service of state sovereignty. Delivering food and medicine is part of a military strategy of bringing peace to a region so as to eliminate the terrorist

---

1. For in-depth analysis of the business of humanitarian aid, see Weiss (2013), who discusses the $18 billion business as of 2011, the way aid agencies train operatives to pose with children for publicity and "disaster pornography" generally, the collaboration between security forces (both government and private) to protect aid workers, and the connection between new humanitarian warfare and humanitarian aid. Overall, he concludes that humanitarian aid has become big business, with agencies competing for markets, planning advertising campaigns, and taking in big bucks in what Naomi Klein (2007) calls "disaster capitalism."

threat at home. In other words, humanitarian space is essential to the war on terror, not only as part of a strategy to shore up the sovereign power of failed states and bring democracy to nations formerly controlled by despots but also to protect Western democracies by preventing the exportation of terrorism from these troubled regions.

If the second phase of humanitarianism was a demand for nongovernmental sovereign humanitarian space, the current phase involves humanitarian agencies working in conjunction with state agencies, including military forces, to replace "failed states" with democratic sovereign states and avoid the humanitarian fallout that leads to terrorism. Human rights are now defined in terms of self-determination for both individuals and states, even while *universal* human rights continue to be at odds with state sovereignty when it comes to refugees from those failed states that are considered threats to national security. In other words, both humanitarian aid and humanitarian warfare work to shore up state sovereignty through relief and military operations in "failed states" like Syria, on one hand, and by containing refugees from those states in camps at the borders of European nations, on the other. Humanitarian aid works with and against state sovereignty, claiming its own sovereignty as neutral, apolitical space, even while it continues to take sides, knowingly or unwittingly.

A deconstructive approach teaches us that we must continue to investigate the ways in which calls for neutral or apolitical space play into conflicts and violence and how sovereignty is always linked to the violence of might makes right, operating according to contradictory logic through which what threatens it is also what saves it, and vice versa. When the threats to it don't destroy national sovereignty, they make it stronger, whether those threats are from international humanitarian organizations, international military forces, or terrorist groups and failed states.

Human Rights Discourse as Alibi for Humanitarian War

RECENTLY, Zygmunt Buaman called the refugee crisis "humanity's crisis," arguing for "the solidarity of humans" capable of mutual love rather than hate or indifference beyond the boundaries of national sovereignty. Yet, philosophers Hannah Arendt and Giorgio Agamben, among others, have challenged abstract concepts of *the human* or *humanity* as apolitical and therefore unable to ground political rights for refugees (e.g., see Halley and Brown 2002, 432–33; see also Rosemont 1991; Kennedy 2002).[1] Taking up the rally

---

1. On refugee rights in particular, see Boehm (2015). It is important to note that neither Arendt nor Agamben considers the gender of refugees when criticizing human rights discourse. And the figure of the refugee that Agamben imagines as the starting point for a new political philosophy is either without gender or assumed to be male. For women refugees, formal equality without attention to gender differences, whether in detention centers or camps, leads to increased gender-based violence, along with lack of medical care and hygiene needs specific to women, which affects women's access to other resources as well (e.g., education, work). In their study of the relation of gender to humanitarian aid, Hilde van Dijkhorst and Suzette Vonhof (2005, 34) found that "a lack of gender awareness in humanitarian aid can lead to many unwanted, even unsafe, situations for women. There is clear evidence that for instance poor thought-out infrastructure of refugee camps can lead to an increased risk of gender-based violence." Feminist theorist Wendy Brown discusses the paradox of women's rights as either basing rights on characteristics specific to feminine or female identity, and

cry for humanity and the human does not mean we are necessarily equipped to ward off violence, inside the camps or outside. The abstract category of human rights, founded in the Enlightenment notion of cosmopolitanism, can even become an alibi for genocide. On the other hand, human rights discourse has been effective and transformative in securing rights for those disenfranchised in many situations.[2] Although we cannot dispense with human rights discourse, we must be vigilant in critically examining how it can be used to justify violence and as an alibi for war.[3]

More than sixty years ago, following her own escape from Nazi Germany, Hannah Arendt identified what she called the paradox of "inalienable human rights" that reduce the person to an "'abstract' human being who seemed to exist nowhere," "independent of all governments." As stateless, there is "no authority, or basis on which to protect" refugees (Arendt 1973, 291–92, 300). Specifically, in the case of Jews fleeing the Holocaust, she says, "Abstract nakedness of being nothing but human was their greatest danger" (Arendt [1943] 1994, 118). Arendt argues that rights are political and therefore a matter of enforceable laws, not abstract conceptions of some supposedly innate quality such as humanity.[4] Nearly a decade earlier, already living in exile in 1943, Arendt

---

thereby reinforcing a subordinated or abjected identity, on one hand, or basing rights on universal characteristics associated with masculine and male identity and thereby continuing to devalue femininity and female identity, on the other. She contends, "The paradox, then, is that rights that entail some specification of our suffering, injury, or inequality lock us into the identity defined by our subordination, and rights that eschew this specificity not only sustain the invisibility of our subordination but potentially even enhance it" (Halley and Brown 2002, 423). For a discussion of human rights discourse in relation to refugee women, see Oliver (forthcoming).

2. For an insightful discussion of the value of human rights discourse, see Meyers (2016).

3. For a discussion of how women's rights in particular have been used to justify war, see Oliver (2007).

4. Recently, following Arendt, David Owen (2016a) has argued that refugees should not be a matter of humanitarian aid but a political responsi-

wrote an essay titled "We Refugees," first published in a small Jewish magazine called *The Menorah Journal*. There Arendt argues that prior to the war, refugees were people who committed acts or held political opinions making them enemies of one state, thus seeking refuge in another. But Jews and others escaping the Nazis had done nothing to challenge their nation-state; they were so-called voluntary exiles with the supposed "choice" (individual sovereignty) to leave and live or stay and die.

These World War II refugees, in response to whom the 1951 UN Refugee Convention protocol was ratified, are akin to contemporary refugees from Syria in that they are not necessarily enemies of the state and they supposedly flee voluntarily. Yet, unlike refugees from the 1950s, today's refugees are not necessarily fleeing "owing to well-found fear of being persecuted for reasons of race, religion, nationality, membership of a particular social group or political opinion," demanded by the 1951 refugee protocol and its 1967 amendments. Instead, they are caught in a war zone in an undeclared war between the Syrian military, ISIS, Russia, the United States, France, the United Kingdom, and others committed to the so-called war on terror. At the very least, these refugees are collateral damage in the war on terror, if not also climate refugees from an increasingly drought- and famine-wrought region.

Arendt argues for a political solution that takes us beyond human rights. And certainly much of what she had to say about her own situation and that of other refugees fleeing Nazi Germany applies to refugees today. For example, she identifies the problematic binary of treating refugees as either threats to be detained (even worse off than criminals in that they are imprisoned without a trial) or charity cases to be saved, often through so-called volun-

---

bility in an international community where states have differing degrees of political responsibility to refugees. Also see Owen (2016c), where he argues that justice requires more than fairness; in particular, he argues that justice may require taking more than one's fair share of refugees on the part of nation-states.

tary internment (Arendt [1943] 1994, 110). And when they aren't interned, refuges are paradoxically considered both "pariahs and parvenus" or social climbers (110).

Closely following Arendt, fifty years later, Giorgio Agamben transforms her notion of abstract nakedness into what he calls "bare life" and argues that there is no place in politics for the concept of the human or rights based on this abstract concept. Like Arendt, he insists that only citizens have rights, and even those rights are linked to this problematic apolitical notion of the human. Proposing to take us beyond human rights, and beyond nation-states, Agamben (2008) claims that the refugee is the central figure for contemporary political philosophy, the figure on which we can build a new community of those who don't belong, beyond borders and frontiers. He says, "It is even possible that, if we want to be equal to the absolutely new tasks ahead, we will have to abandon decidedly, without reservation, the fundamental concepts through which we have so far represented the subjects of the political (Man, the Citizen and its rights, but also the sovereign people, the worker, and so forth) and build our political philosophy anew starting from the one and only figure of the refugee" (90). The problem these philosophers identify is not with human rights per se but rather with the depoliticization of human rights insofar as the notion of the human remains fluid or undefined, which is not to say that it cannot also be a useful category in politics.

Although, like Arendt and Agamben, Jacques Derrida is critical of human rights and state sovereignty, he demonstrates how, within Western thought, the human operates as the flip side of the sovereign citizen. He shows how the category "human" has always been political, part and parcel of the politics of naming. He shows how humanity and sovereignty are traditionally, conceptually, and politically linked (in particular, see Derrida 2008; 2009a). Furthermore, he argues that the concept of the human already includes what it defines itself against, namely, the animal, the machine, the beast, the sovereign. As Agamben provocatively suggests, then, beginning with the figure of the refugee may turn political philosophy on its head, but it still leaves in place the binary opposition citizen–refugee. Rather than merely replace the dominant side of a binary opposition with its underside, Derrida works to deconstruct the opposition on which binary hierarchies depend, and he does so from within the philosophical, political, and literary traditions we have inherited—or to put it in more Derridean terms, that we *will have* inherited, since the past is not a thing lying there to be found but rather a kernel of the future (the to-come) that shakes the foundations of what we take to be our world.

Derrida repeatedly demonstrates that the designation *human* is always political insofar as, historically, the names "humanity" and "human" have operated as exclusionary categories, based on a dangerous notion of sovereignty that reasserts itself with more force in those moments when it is undermined or under scrutiny, as it is now with the massive influx of refugees in the Middle East, Europe, and Africa. As Derrida points out, the category of the human or humanity has been used to justify killing, even genocide. Indeed, insofar as the category operates as an exclusionary category, it is part and parcel of a logic of genocide. As we know, genocide is typically justified by identifying the target group with animals, subhumans, or inferior beings. Derrida reminds us that human rights discourses inherit this questionable and problematic history wherein the category "human" was (and continues to be) used to justify oppression, torture, and murder.

In 2002, speaking of the way human rights discourse was used as an alibi in NATO's response to violence in Serbia, Derrida said,

> We must deconstruct *ad infinitum* but also denounce the machinations, ruses, lies through which this respectable discourse of human rights accommodates, in an unjust and selective fashion, the hegemonic aims of state-nationalist superpowers. These superpowers do not renounce their own sovereignty. As soon as it seems opportune for them, they do not even respect any longer the organizations of international law that they institute and continue to dominate. (Derrida 2009b, 127)

Certainly this opportunist approach to international law is evident in today's covert international military operation's "rules of engagement," which are not sanctioned by the UN.

In that same lecture, Derrida questions the separation of humanitarian missions from government interests: "precisely where one claims to be acting in the name of humanitarian and human rights principles that are superior to the sovereignty of states, precisely where one grants oneself the right of intervention in the name of human rights, where one judges or intends to judge the authors of war crimes or crimes against humanity, it would be easy to show that this humanitarianism, which cares little about so many other examples of 'ethnic cleansing' going on in the world, still remains, and brutally so, in the service of state interests of all kinds (economic or strategic), whether they are interests shared by the NATO allies, or even in dispute between them (for example between the United States and Europe)" (Derrida 2009b, 125–26). There are, of course, so many examples of this disparate caring. For just one case, take disparities between Western media reactions to refugees arriving in Europe and to the deaths of refugees at sea on their way to Greece or Italy, Western media coverage of refugees fleeing civil war in Africa and of the recent announcement of plans to close the largest refugee camp in the world, Dadaab, which "houses" more than three hundred thousand people on Kenya's border. Another example, mentioned earlier, is the exodus of women refugees from Central America who seek asylum in Mexico and the United States; these refugees get very little media attention. In a world where the lives of some matter more than the lives of others, genocidal logics always loom on the horizon. Humanitarian aid becomes an alibi for the lack of a political solution in the war on terror, a war without an easily identifiable enemy.

Recall the Bush administration's use of the rhetoric of women's rights to justify invasions of Afghanistan and Iraq. Women's rights, and human rights more generally, have often been used as justification for wars of so-called liberation.[5] Another striking example of the collusion of human rights discourse and the justification of war, killing, and even torture is the current textbook for U.S. counterinsurgency, the one used in Baghdad and Afghanistan, which was co-sponsored by the director of Harvard's Carr Center for Human Rights, who helped draft the manual. According to Eyal Weizman (2011, 17), "in her introduction to the Chicago University Press version of the manual, [Sarah] Sewall [then director] announced it as the product of an 'unprecedented collaboration [between] a human rights center partnered with the armed forces' that focused on reducing collateral damage as a military tactic." Reducing loss of life is a human rights issue but has become a military issue insofar as it is also strategically advantageous in winning a war.

According to Weizman, former general Stanley McChrystal "was one of the manual's most devoted followers" and saw his military objective not in terms of "seizing terrain or destroying insurgent forces" but in terms of "population" by limiting civilian causalities and collateral damage (18). One military historian went so far as to say that contemporary warfare is "social work with guns" (18). But, as Weizman points out, the "utilitarian use of humanitarian and human rights principles must acknowledge the possibility of its inverse and the speed by which such inversions occur. If protecting civilians is used as a way of convincing people to comply with military government, at other times inflicting pain on them might usefully achieve the same ends" (18).

This new "humanitarian" warfare uses the calculus of collateral damage in conjunction with human rights discourse as a contemporary weapon of war. In the words of Derrida (2005, 46), in these cases, "a discourse on human rights and on democracy remains little more than an obscene alibi so long as it tolerates the terrible

---

5. For a sustained analysis of the use of women's rights to justify war, see Oliver (2007).

plight of so many millions of human beings suffering from malnutrition, disease, and humiliation, grossly deprived not only of bread and water but of equality or freedom, dispossessed of the rights of all, of everyone, of anyone."

Collateral Damage and the Lesser of Evils

THE DISCOURSE OF COLLATERAL DAMAGE, then, is not only over-taking the human rights discourse but also incorporating it and using it to justify so-called humanitarian warfare. Within this log-ic of utilitarian calculus of risk–benefit analysis, refugees are num-bers to be plugged into complicated equations to assess the bene-fits of helping them, primarily in terms of the safety and security of the so-called host nations. Even humanitarian aid organizations such as Doctors without Borders now employ risk management personnel charged with calculating the risks and benefits of giving aid (see Neuman and Weissman 2016). These calculations cannot account for the singularity of individuals and their experiences; nor do they factor in human dignity or respect or the basic quality of life. Within this calculus, refugees become exchangeable, fungi-ble, and eventually disposable.

For example, Turkey's membership into the European Union is contingent on the nation taking a certain quota of refugees. Ongoing negotiations between the EU and Turkey revolve around how much money the EU will provide in exchange for each ref-ugee and whether Turkish citizens will be able to move freely within the EU, even while the freedom of movement of refugees is severely restricted and circumscribed. Closer to home, the U.S. government is paying Mexico to keep refugees from Central

America from crossing the border to seek asylum. The United States has "outsourced" the refugee problem to Mexico, where most asylum seekers are either detained for long periods in rat-infested jails eating worm-infested food or deported to face violence or death back at home (see Nazario 2015). Refugees have become disposable insofar as their lives, safety, and security, along with their freedom of movement, are exchanged for both money and the freedom of movement of others.

Refugees have become collateral damage in civil wars and the so-called war on terror, when they aren't pawns to be exchanged in negotiations between governments. In this new form of warfare, international military forces organized by state officials, and operating according to international "rules of engagement," are no longer necessarily tied to national constitutions or declarations of war. These operations are often designed to minimize "collateral damage." This form of international warfare, without a front line, without a clear enemy, without a formal declaration of war, without judicial approval, seemingly beyond nation-states, is fought in the name of national security and protecting citizens. Yet, American and European nationals carry out terror attacks from inside state borders, where "hotbeds" of religious fanaticism supposedly spawned in Afghanistan, Iraq, or Syria are actually sprouting and growing in Florida flight schools or Brussels suburbs. Smart bombs and surgical strikes supposedly limit the loss of life, while computer programs are used to calculate collateral damage in the name of a more humane killing. And the military follows "rules of engagement" agreed upon by our allies, designed not only to limit loss of life but also to limit liability, particularly legal liability or liability to media scandals.

These rules of engagement are based on calculations of proportionality in which computer models perform risk–benefit analyses to assess what targets are worth and what collateral damage is acceptable. Humanitarian aid figures into these calculations insofar as military strategy includes shoring up the sovereignty of so-called failed states by considering issues of poverty and famine insofar as they are causes of state failure and the radicalization of terrorists, using human rights discourse to cover over calculations of the risks of poor and hungry people becoming terrorists. Contemporary warfare waged by superpowers looks more like targeted assassination justified by complex utilitarian calculations of what deaths are worth more than which lives. In the words of Daniel Resiner, former head of the International Law Division of the Israeli military,

> proportionality is a complex logic with many variables—but how do you compare these? There is no choice but to ask the question, compare and calculate. Proportionality does not tell us what to include in the calculation, what is the equation and what is the exchange rate? . . . Does one dead child equal one dead grownup, or does he equal five grownups? As a lawyer I need numbers to work with. I need thresholds in order to instruct the soldiers. Any number could become a useful benchmark. But when the ground of the law is shaking I am also unstable. (Weizman 2011, 13)

As a lawyer, Resiner is uneasy with the aftershocks of this earthquake in our conception of tolerance, which defines and quantifies how much suffering we can tolerate in terms of proportional logics and the lesser of evils. Tolerance becomes a matter of benchmarks and thresholds wherein "any number" will do as long as there is a clear cutoff between what we can and what we cannot tolerate. The new war craves precision. Surgical strikes, rules of engagement, and computer formulas for acceptable risks and tolerable collateral damage are part of the fantasy of precision and accuracy that privileges quantity over quality, not only to justify violence, but also to disavow the pain and suffering it causes. Within the formula of collateral damage, containing violence and suffering becomes an alibi for more violence and suffering in calculations based on arbitrary thresholds of death assigned by government agencies and the military. Who will die, and how, is calculated using computer programs similar to those used by corporations to project profit margins or by insurance companies to project risk. Statistical analysis replaces ethics or politics as the basis for assessing "just war."

The impossibility of predicting the future, risks or benefits, is disavowed by the fervent adherence to models for calculation that create the illusion of control, mastery, and measure, all in the name of preventing the "worst" violence. Military analysts weigh their options based on calculable measurements of how much violence and death they expect given different possible scenarios. Invoking these calculations, international "peacekeeping" forces justify their killing and oppose it to the irrational, incalculable killing of terrorists. Western forces claim to operate according to the rules of war, now defined in economic terms, while terrorists supposedly don't play by the rules. Even as international military forces continue to make and change the rules in this war without end, front, or declaration, they claim their adherence to rational, principled, measured rules of engagement wherein thresholds of collateral damage and computer programs replace ethical reflection. Within this economic model, the lesser of evils is fewer collateral deaths and more terrorist deaths, calculated with the greatest precision. Of course, reports of civilian causalities and mistakenly bombed hospitals or schools destroy the myth of precision and accuracy in surgical strikes and drone warfare. Even so, within the logic of collateral damage, international military forces can supposedly avoid the "worst."

Certainly since World War II, the "worst" has been associated with the genocide of the Holocaust, if not also with the shadow of annihilation wrought by nuclear bombs dropped on Japan. Following the logic of contemporary warfare, the worst is seen as incalculable violence unleashed outside of any equation of exchange or rational utilitarian principle for measurement. Weizman (2011, 12) argues that contemporary warfare's lesser-of-evils model claims to avoid the worst "by opening a field of equivalence, in which different forms of potential and actual violence, risk, and damage become exchangeable, proportionality approximates an algorithmic logic of computation," wherein the computer becomes the paragon of ethics by removing human sentimentality. Within this logic, reason is reduced to calculation, and ethics becomes computation. Indeterminacy, undecidability, and personal responsibility are evacuated from this fantasy of calculability. And the right thing to do is determined by an answering machine rather than by an ethical or properly political response.

Rethinking the "Worst"

CALCULATION BECOMES AN ALIBI for continued violence, killing, and warfare. "Just war" becomes nothing more than an arbitrary threshold for collateral damage, a number—any number—assigned by military lawyers making, and changing, the rules of engagement as they go along. Reason is reduced to rationale. Ethics is reduced to computation. Politics is reduced to statistical models of population control. And the fantasy of calculability covers over the reality of unpredictability and experiences out of our control. In Derridean language, economic calculation replaces ethical decision. Whether discussing the ethics of hospitality or the politics of democracy, Derrida insists on the impossibility of calculation, even as we calculate (see Derrida 2005, 48, 149; cf. Derrida 2013). When calculation completely eclipses the incalculable, however, and every other is reduced to its countability and exchangeability, we risk replacing an ethical response with a computing machine and rendering responsibility nothing more than account-ability. While Derrida insists that the calculable and incalculable are locked into a necessarily aporetic relationship, his analysis of the "war on terror" suggests that when ethics and politics become nothing more than adding machines, we risk the worst violence rather than avoiding it. Measuring the "worst" is itself part of an economy of hierarchal valuations intended to engage in comparative judgments of which war or whose violence is worse, which killing or massacre is worse.

On one reading of Derrida, the "worst" is associated with the "most" of sovereignty in the logic of might makes right (see Derrida 2009a, 213–14). Within a notion of sovereignty that demands indivisibility, absolute power, and self-control (if not also self-certainty), any and all others (foreigners) are threats. Derrida describes the undemocratic response of democracy through which it tries to protect itself by killing off, or quarantining, those others that might threaten it. The incarceration or detention of refugees is an example of what he calls the autoimmune logic of democracy wherein, in the name of democracy, we justify undemocratic policies.[1] In a world without a clear enemy, however, where every other becomes a possible threat, this autoimmune response risks genocide.

In the words of Derrida scholar Leonard Lawler (2014), "today, the number of 'enemies' is potentially unlimited. *Every* other is wholly other . . . and thus every single other needs to be rejected by the immune system. This innumerable rejection resembles a genocide or what is worse an absolute threat." Another Derrida scholar, Samir Haddad, describes how the notion of the "worst" evolves in Derrida's thought from total nuclear war and the final solution to the autoimmune logic of the archive within which the worst is not just mass killing but also erasure of the trace of an archive through either absolute annihilation of a people and its past or the suffocation of one archive with another (see Haddad 2013, 85–87). While neither of these operations can eliminate all traces of the others or of a people, their logics are genocidal in their attempt to do so. The worst goes beyond literal killing and signals the erasure a way of seeing the world—or we might as well say a world itself—by covering it over with another world-

1. For his part, Derrida (2005) gives the example of suspended elections in Algeria when it was clear that the nondemocratic candidates would win: "They decided in a sovereign fashion to suspend, at least provisionally, democracy *for its own good,* so as to take care of it, so as to immunize it against a much worse and very likely assault" (19).

view. In this regard, comparative models that reduce life to units to be exchanged or plugged into equations operate according to a world-destroying genocidal logic. This is to say, when the "worst" becomes part of the economy of "lesser of evils," life and death are reduced to a logic of calculation that makes them fungible; one life is weighed against another, one war against another: which is worse (and therefore risks the worst), ethnic cleansing in Bosnia or the Nazi death camps? Which is worse, killing one little girl or killing three soldiers? And so on. Within the calculus of collateral damage, the worst is reduced to the worse, and everything imaginable is also calculable.

Whatever Derrida does or doesn't say about the worst, the worst "worthy of its name" must remain outside this economy of exchange, an impossible condition of possibility for thinking of what is better or worse, the incalculable always in tension with what can be calculated. As Derrida suggests in his final seminar, the death of each and every person, each and every living being, is not just the end of a world but the end of the world.[2] If genocide is the destruction of a world through killing and erasure of archives, then the hundreds of thousands of people literally corralled into the camp "refugee" are victims of genocide. Derrida (1984, 28) claims, "There is no common measure adequate to persuade me that a personal mourning is less serious than a nuclear war." And once we think there is, we start on the slippery slope of utilitarian calculus and exclusionary line drawing that risk genocide.

Statistical models that compute comparative valuations risk the "worst" insofar as they set out a hierarchy of life, human and otherwise, through which violence is justified, where some lives are valuable (in this case, citizens' lives) while others are disposable (in this case, refugees' lives). Within the logic of contemporary "humanitarian" warfare, the worst is considered a war without

2. For a discussion of what Derrida means by the end of "the world," see Oliver (2015) and Naas (2014).

rules—that is to say, without limits on collateral damage. To the contrary, the rationale of collateral damage and proportionality through which lives are reduced to numbers, quantified, and compared for relative value or disposability operates according to a genocidal logic that risks the "worst." Once we imagine the worst, we can do it, and then we can imagine something even worse. For the worst to operate as a limit to our imaginations, it must remain impossible, forever at odds with the genocidal logic of collateral damage and risk–benefit analysis.

A New Form of Genocide

BY ALL ACCOUNTS, Raphael Lemkin, a Polish–Jewish lawyer who fled Nazi Germany to the United States during World War II, first used the term *genocide*. Rather than limit genocide to mass murder, Lemkin's (2005, 79) definition includes "the destruction of the personal security, liberty, health, dignity, and even the lives of the individuals belonging to [national] groups." As we have seen, following Lemkin, the UN Genocide Convention cites debilitating living conditions, wherein a genocidal act can include "deliberate deprivation of resources needed for the group's physical survival and which are available to the rest of the population, such as clean water, food and medical services; Creation of circumstances that could lead to a slow death, such as lack of proper housing, clothing and hygiene or excessive work or physical exertion" (Office of the UN Special Adviser on the Prevention of Genocide, n.d.). In these terms, the treatment of refugees fleeing civil wars and violence in Syria, the Sudan, and many other regions meets the criteria of genocide insofar as the refugees' living conditions in camps and detention centers are certainly lacking in personal security, liberty, health, and dignity and also too are often lacking in clean water, food and medical services, proper housing, clothing, and hygiene and lead to sickness, disease, and death. Thousands of refugees die every year trying to escape violence at home; and the ones who make it too often encounter violence in their "host" country.

Civil war and violence, along with famine and drought, have led to mass migrations of people fleeing for their lives (UNHCR 2015a). Refugees make up a significant subgroup of the global population subject to incarceration and deprivation and, ultimately, to the genocidal logic of contemporary international military policies governing border security.

The refugee has become a global category that includes millions of people worldwide. Along with civil war, famine, and violence at home, the insistence on border patrols, national security, and the protection of certain citizens over others has created the "refugee crisis" wherein most of these displaced people lack proper shelter, clothing, and food; they lack the basic necessities of life. On the international stage, the category "refugee" operates according to a genocidal logic insofar as it produces a group of disposable people whose lives are marginal. In other words, international policy operates according to a genocidal logic that creates a group of people called "refugees," who, if not outright murdered, are let—or even made—to die, whether from drowning, disease, starvation, or lack of health care. If refugees constitute a group, then as a group, they are denied the most basic necessities of life. Moreover, the logic of international policies toward refugees is genocidal insofar as it renders refugees fungible and disposable: figuratively as collateral damage in the war against terrorism and literally as they are exchanged as bargaining chips in international agreements between the United States and Mexico, for example, or Germany and the European Union and Turkey. Insofar as refugees have become a global subset of the human population, and insofar as they have become "collateral damage" in this age of humanitarian warfare, their lives are treated as fungible and disposable.

Currently human rights discourse has become comingled with risk–benefit analysis, which is part and parcel of a genocidal logic. Within the logic of risk–benefit, reducing life to statistical models and calculating costs and benefits become alibis for a seemingly more humanitarian warfare. Designed to avoid the worst violence (traditionally equated with genocide) by embracing the lesser of evils, the utilitarian cost–benefit model actually risks the worst violence. The calculus itself risks turning human life, or all life, into exchangeable units. This economy in which human life becomes fungible operates according to a genocidal logic in which the lives of some have become disposable. Indeed, statistical proportional analysis of collateral damage is part and parcel of genocidal logic defined as a view of human life (or nonhuman life) that leads to the practice of making one subset of that population fungible or disposable.[1] Refugees are a population that has been made fungible and disposable.

1. While some may find my definition of genocide too broad, even in its inception, genocide referred to much more than mass murder. Here are some examples of attempts to define genocide that take us beyond mass murder: "genocide is the extent of destruction of a social collectivity by whatever agents, with whatever intentions, by purposive actions which fall outside the recognized conventions of legitimate warfare" (Thompson and Quets 1987, 17); "genocide is the deliberate, organized destruction, in whole or in large part, of racial or ethnic groups by a government or its agents. It can involve not only mass murder, but also forced deportation (ethnic cleansing), systematic rape, and economic and biological subjugation" (Shaw 2015, 34; cf. Dobkowski and Wallimann 1989); "genocide is any act that puts the very existence of a group in jeopardy" (Midlarsky 2005; see also Levene 2005).

Humanitarian Aid as
Poison and Cure

ON A DAILY BASIS, international humanitarian aid organizations and international military forces engage in calculations of life and death, weighing the lives of some against the lives of others, the risks of taking in refugees versus the risks of refusing them, calculations designed to determine how much suffering is tolerable. Tolerance, from the Latin *tolerare*, "to tolerate," means to endure, especially something painful. In the utilitarian calculus of humanitarian war, pain and suffering are no longer qualities or capacities that define humanity but rather quantities plugged into equations of life and death. *How much* suffering we can *tolerate* becomes weighing the "lesser of evils" in an economy of exchange, proportionality, and collateral damage. Tolerance has always been a matter of endurance—how much pain and suffering we can tolerate. Only now, tolerance is measured, quantified, and calculated using the latest computer models and sophisticated risk–benefit rubrics.

"Tolerance," says Derrida, "is actually the opposite of hospitality" (Borradori 2003, 127). Unconditional hospitality does not calculate or quantify but rather opens itself up to what comes from opening doors and windows and exposing oneself to the threshold: "Supposing that we dwelled on the threshold, we would also have to endure the ordeal of feeling the *earthquake* always under way, threatening the existence of every threshold, threatening both its indivisibility and its foundational solidity" (Derrida 2009b, 413, emphasis added)—that is to say, threatening the sovereignty of the subject or citizen, and the state or nation, and of any and every body that takes itself to be self-determined and autonomous, and therefore immune to suffering. As it is, humanitarian aid that leaves refugees locked in camps and detention centers, barely able to survive, hardly counts as tolerance, let alone hospitality. Camps are places of containment, not welcome, in a world where is it becoming more and more difficult to distinguish humanitarian aid from humanitarian warfare.

Derrida (2006, 106) describes the role of what he calls the "philosopher-deconstructor" as analyzing "the practical and effective consequences of the relationship between our philosophical heritage and the structure of the [still] dominant juridico-political system, even as it is undergoing mutation [even as an earthquake is transforming the landscape], not in order to justify it, but in order to comprehend it." As he says, one can describe and explain associations and events that "lead to war or terrorism without justifying them in the least, while in fact condemning them and attempting to invent other associations" (Derrida 2006, 106). Conversely, one can critically engage human rights, humanitarian aid, and humanitarian space without condemning them, perhaps even endorsing them, while issuing a warning about the ways in which they play into the hands of the very systems that perpetuate continued violence and suffering.

Conclusion: Toward
Hospitality as Earth Ethics

THIS EARTHQUAKE in the landscape of tolerance shakes up our worldview. Elsewhere, I have associated earth with ethics and world with politics, and the necessarily tense relation between them as the space of justice (see Oliver 2015). We must move beyond mere tolerance and toward ethical and political responsibility. Taking up the earthquake metaphor running through this book, a just political approach to the refugee crisis requires a new ethical approach to sharing the planet. We must move beyond both rescue politics and carceral humanitarianism, which entails moving beyond fenced and walled national borders. To do so, we must reconceive of our relationships to other people who share planet earth, beyond citizenship and national identity. Furthermore, we must think of our obligations to others not just in terms of human rights or humanitarian aid but also in terms of radical hospitality and responsibility as response to those in need. In conclusion, I turn to Derrida's conception of unconditional hospitality, and his distinction between visitation and invitation, to begin to rethink our obligations to asylum seekers beyond detention centers and refugee camps. In the end, I propose an earth ethics wherein our obligations are based on our common planetary home rather than on our national or individual homes. Rather than see ourselves as Americans or Europeans, offering aid to others less fortunate, we should see ourselves as earthlings sharing the planet. Rather than a rescue politics that requires perilous escape and lifeboat scenarios, we should consider our ethical obligations beyond national borders and beyond mere physical proximity. Once we consider our position in relation to others from an earthly perspective, we can no longer deny our interdependence and our shared dependence on each other and our planetary home.

Those familiar with Derrida's notion of unconditional hospitality know that he sets it against Kant's cosmopolitan notion of limited or conditioned hospitality.[1] Kant articulates a right to limited hospitality of a guest, particularly in the context of commercial trade.[2] Derrida insists that true or just hospitality must be without conditions or limits. He opposes just hospitality to hospitality by right, which is always limited.[3] For him, hospitality always

1. For example, against Kant's limited hospitality, Derrida (2000, 14) argues, "At bottom, before even beginning, we could end our reflections here in the formalization of a law of hospitality which violently imposes a contradiction on the very concept of hospitality in fixing a limit to it, in determining it: hospitality is certainly, necessarily, a right, a duty, an obligation, the *greeting* of the foreign other [*l'autre étranger*] as a friend but on the condition that the host, the *Wirt,* the one who receives, lodges or *gives asylum* remains the *patron,* the master of the household, on the condition that he maintains his own authority *in his own home,* that he looks after himself and sees to and considers all that concerns him [*qu'il se garde et garde et regarde ce qui le regarde*] and thereby affirms the law of hospitality as the law of the household, *oikonomia,* the law of his household, the law of a place (house, hotel, hospital, hospice, family, city, nation, language, etc.), the law of identity which de-limits the *very* place of proffered hospitality and maintains authority over it, maintains the truth of authority, remains the place of this maintaining, which is to say, of truth, thus limiting the gift proffered and making of this limitation, namely, the *being-oneself in one's own home,* the condition of the gift and of hospitality."
2. For a sustained discussion of Kant's notion of hospitality and Derrida's criticisms of it, see Oliver (2015).
3. For example, he says, "The law of absolute hospitality commands a break with hospitality by right, with law or justice as rights. Just hospitality breaks with hospitality by right; not that it condemns or is opposed to it, and it can on the contrary set and maintain it in a perpetual progressive

operates between these two poles of the unconditional (the ethical demand) and the conditional (the political reality).[4] Justice is always on the horizon of this tension between the unconditional and the conditional, not only because justice is always deferred but also because of the inherent conflict between the concept of unconditional hospitality and the realities of limited hospitality. The gap between the two is so great, Derrida suggests, we don't even understand or know what hospitality is, in large part because hospitality is not just a matter of understanding or knowledge; it is not, contra Kant, just a matter of categorical imperatives, duties, and reason but also of compassion, desire, and a certain "madness" Derrida associates with Kierkegaard's madness of impossible faith. In fact, Derrida claims that as soon as we identify the guest as foreigner (or refugee), we've already done him violence by reducing him to a category that we think we understand. Furthermore, by questioning him, we continue our violence, not only because we may do so in a language unknown to him, and because we most likely are interrogating him in an unfamiliar legal process, but also because we are calling on him to account for himself and there-

movement; but it is as strangely heterogeneous to it as justice is heterogeneous to the law to which it is yet so close, from which in truth it is indissociable" (Derrida and Dufourmantelle 2000, 25, 27).

4. For example, Derrida says, "We will always be threatened by this dilemma between, on the one hand, unconditional hospitality that dispenses with law, duty, or even politics, and, on the other, hospitality circumscribed by law and duty. One of them can always corrupt the other, and this capacity for perversion remains irreducible. It must remain so" (Derrida and Dufourmantelle 2000, 135). Consider also this passage: "It is a question of knowing how to transform and improve the law, and of knowing if this improvement is possible within an historical space which takes place *between* the Law of an unconditional hospitality, ordered *a priori* to every other, to all newcomers, *whoever they may be,* and *the* conditional laws of a right to hospitality, without which *The* unconditional Law of hospitality would be in danger of remaining a pious and irresponsible desire, without form and without potency, and of even being perverted at any moment" (Derrida 2001, 22–23).

by subjecting him to our assumed superior judgment.[5] Insofar as hospitality is the opening of the home or ethos, it is not simply one obligation among others; rather, "hospitality is culture itself and not simply one ethic amongst others. Insofar as it has to do with the *ethos,* that is, the residence, one's home, the familiar place of dwelling, inasmuch as it is a manner of being there, the manner in which we relate to ourselves and to others, to others as our own or as foreigners, *ethics is hospitality*; ethics is so thoroughly coextensive with the experience of hospitality" (Derrida 2001, 16–17; cf. Derrida and Dufourmantelle 2000, 149, 151).

This is to say, the ethos of our cohabitation is at stake, and conversely, cohabitation on our shared planet is a matter of ethics/ethos of home.[6] When we broaden our perspective to that of the earth and those with whom we share the earth, when we think of home in relation to ethics and politics, it becomes clear that everyone belongs and has a right to home. All mammals, humans included, need a safe place to sleep at night. This is precisely what refugees lack. We could contrast the political realities of homelessness and the lack of sleep with the ethical insomnia Derrida (following Levinas) associates with ethics. Both Levinas and Derrida repeat-

---

5. For example, Derrida (2000, 8) argues, "Hospitality is owed to the other as stranger. But if one determines the other as stranger, one is already introducing the circles of conditionality that are family, nation, state, and citizenship. . . . It is doubtless necessary to know all that can be known of hospitality, and there is much to know; it is certainly necessary to bring this knowledge to the highest and fullest consciousness possible; but it is also necessary to know that hospitality gives itself, and gives itself to thought beyond knowledge." Consider also this passage: "The foreigner is first of all foreign to the legal language in which the duty of hospitality is formulated, the right to asylum, its limits, norms, policing, etc. He has to ask for hospitality in a language which by definition is not his own, the one imposed on him by the master of the house, the host, the king, the lord, the authorities, the nation, the State, the father, etc. This personage imposes on him translation into their own language, and that's the first act of violence" (Derrida and Dufourmantelle 2000, 15).

6. For a discussion of earth ethics in relation to the home, see Oliver (2015).

edly use the metaphor of insomnia to stress the urgency of the ethical obligations to others. Our ethical responsibility should keep us awake at night and make us vigilant. Ethics can never sleep. But, what do we make of this ethical sleeplessness when considering the harsh realities of refugee sleeplessness? Here again, the tension between politics and ethics shows itself. A safe place to sleep requires doors and windows; and yet, when we close those doors and windows to others, we turn our backs on the ethical call from those in need.

Derrida identifies a paradox at the heart of hospitality between the need for a home with doors and windows, fences and borders—that is to say, limits—and the openness required by unconditional hospitality. To be a host, one must have a home. Yet, as Derrida describes it, hospitality requires a reversal between host and guest such that the host becomes almost a hostage to his guest. His hyperbolic account of hospitality points to the assumptions of mastery and sovereignty already operating in our everyday notions of hospitality, particularly when it comes to welcoming foreigners and refugees, that as soon as there are doors and windows, someone holds their keys (Derrida 2000, 14).

Certainly national sovereignty is part and parcel of the law of hospitality, particularly as it is set out in international law concerning refugees and asylum seekers. And, as Derrida argues, national sovereignty is always in an "autoimmune" relationship with democracy. In terms of hospitality, this means that not only is there a conflict between the concept and practice of hospitality but also the concept of hospitality itself operates according to an autoimmune logic: "Hospitality is a self-contradictory concept and experience which can only self-destruct, put otherwise, produce itself as impossible, only be possible on the condition of its impossibility, or protect itself from itself, autoimmunize itself in some way, which is to say, deconstruct itself—precisely—in being put into practice" (5). Derrida drives home the problems with our everyday notions of hospitality with his distinction between the *hospitality of invitation* and the *hospitality of visitation*: "In visitation there is no door. Anyone can come at any time and can come in without needing a key for the door. There are no customs checks with a visitation. But there are customs and police checks with an invitation" (14). The hospitality of invitation is a limited, controlled, monitored hospitality, whereas the hospitality of visitation is unconditional hospitality, which is not controlled by the host. The visitor arrives uninvited, unexpected, unknown, and perhaps even unwelcomed; and yet the host has an ethical obligation that comes from a hospitality of justice (rather than merely of rights) to take her in, even if her presence threatens our way of life: "a visitation could be an invasion by the worst. Unconditional hospitality must remain open without horizon of expectation, without anticipation, to any surprise visitation" (17). Derrida's radical hospitality suggests that to avoid the "worst"—the worst violence—we must allow the possibility of the worst to enter. This is the autoimmune logic of hospitality. It must always remain open to what comes, for better or worse. And while our practices of hospitality can never live up to this ideal, without holding on to the concept of just unconditional, impossible hospitality, our everyday practices of hospitality are hollow, illusions of hospitality and self-deception at best, or alibis for continued violence at worst.

In light of Derrida's standard of unconditional, or just, hospitality, the carceral humanitarian aid of refugee camps and detention centers falls far short. Indeed, camps and lockups hardly meet the basic criteria for limited, conditional hospitality. For, with very few exceptions, it's difficult to use the word *hospitality* to describe the situation of most refugees and asylum seekers when they arrive at the borders of their host countries, which have barely begun to provide even for the basic needs of refugees and asylum seekers or to provide the basic human rights supposedly guaranteed by international conventions. What would it mean, then, to think beyond rights discourse, beyond borders, beyond detention centers and refugee camps, and toward justice as radical hospitality? First, and foremost, we would have to move beyond notions of national sovereignty and citizenship. Rather than starting with human rights, or citizen's rights, as the basis of political (or ethical) obligations, we would have to acknowledge our interdependence on this shared planet, our only home. Rather than claim the sovereign right to welcome others into our own homes, we would have to acknowledge that the foundation for that home is the earth itself, which belongs to us not as property but rather as what we share with every other earthling. In other words, the grounds for our claiming any home at all is the home we all share, planet earth. Insofar as climate change and climate displacement exacerbate, if not cause, most forced migration on the planet today, we need to come to terms with the fact that earth is our only home, and therefore we have an obligation to it, and to those with whom we share the planet.

Some "climatologists say Syria is a grim preview of what could be in store for the larger Middle East, the Mediterranean and other parts of the world. The drought, they maintain, was exacerbated by climate change. . . . Syria's drought has destroyed crops, killed livestock and displaced as many as 1.5 million Syrian farmers. In the process, it touched off the social turmoil that burst into civil war" (Wendle 2015; see also Kelley et al. 2015). In the last seven years, an estimated one person every second has been displaced by a disaster, and that number is on the rise thanks to climate change and poor design and planning (see Displacement Monitoring Center 2015). There is evidence that climate change plays a central role in mass migrations in Africa and has led to hundreds of thousands in refugee camps (see Schwartzstein 2016; Hrala 2016). The problem of climate refugees is only going to get worse. And international law and UN guidelines do not consider those escaping natural disasters and drought or climate change refugees. Can we say that people fleeing drought and famine, or flooding and receding shores, in their homelands are being persecuted? If so, by whom?

These questions make clear the need to rethink refugees beyond identity politics that requires one group at war with another or the persecution of one group by another. Earth ethics requires us to begin to think of ourselves, and our relation to each other, beyond group or national identities and toward interrelationality determined by the interconnectedness of ecosystems and our biosphere. As I've argued elsewhere, we need to embrace an earth ethics as a response ethics through which we consider our obligations to others as obligations to ourselves, and vice versa, for our very survival depends on it (Oliver 2015). We need to respond to others in ways that open up, rather than close down, the possibility of response.

In terms of refugees and asylum seekers, whether they are escaping the violence of civil war, natural disasters, or climate change, they should not be detained, incarcerated, or locked into camps but rather at least be granted the rights coming to them under international law and, moreover, the ethical responsibility owed to them as fellow inhabitants of our earthly home. As we have seen, current conditions in refugee camps and detention centers violate some basic human rights supposedly guaranteed by international law and UN conventions on refugees and asylum seekers. More than this, rescue politics and carceral humanitarian create an impossible subject position for the "refugee," which simultaneously requires and undermines both national and individual sovereignty. Incarcerating and interning refugees is not only politically wrong in terms of our own standards set out by the UN but also ethically wrong in terms of our obligations to each other as coinhabitants of our shared planetary home.

References

Al Jazeera. 2016. "Hundreds of Refugees Died on Way to Europe This Year." February 9. http://www.aljazeera.com/news/2016/02/400 -refugees-die-europe-2016-160209133941502.html.

Agamben, Giorgio. 2008. "Beyond Human Rights." *Social Engineering* 15: 90–95.

Arendt, Hannah. 1943 (1994). "We Refugees." In *Altogether Elsewhere: Writers in Exile,* edited by Marc Robinson, 110–19. Boston: Faber and Faber.

——. (1964) 2003. "Personal Responsibility under Dictatorship." In *Responsibility and Judgment,* edited by Jerome Kohne, 17–48. New York: Schoken Books.

——. 1973. *The Origins of Totalitarianism*. Orlando, Fla.: Harcourt, Brace, Jovanovich.

Baillot, Helen, Sharon Cowan, and Vanessa E. Munro. 2009. "Seen but Not Heard? Parallels and Dissonances in the Treatment of Rape Narratives across the Asylum and Criminal Justice Contexts." *Journal of Law and Society* 36, no. 2: 195–219.

——. 2013. "'Hearing the Right Gaps': Enabling and Responding to Disclosures of Sexual Violence within the UK Asylum Process." *Social and Legal Studies* 21: 269–96.

Barnett, Michael. 2013. *Empire of Humanity: A History of Humanitarianism*. Ithaca, N.Y.: Cornell University Press.

BBC News. 2016. "Migrant Crisis: Migration to Europe Explained in Seven Charts." Last modified March 4. http://www.bbc.com/news/world -europe-34131911.

Boehm, Omri. 2015. "Can Refugees Have Human Rights?" *The Stone* (blog), October 19. http://opinionator.blogs.nytimes.com/author/omri -boehm/?_r=0.

Borradori, Giovanna. 2003. *Philosophy in a Time of Terror: Dialogues with Jacques Derrida and Jürgen Habermas*. Chicago: University of Chicago Press.

Brown, Wendy. 2014. *Walled States, Waning Sovereignty.* Cambridge: Zone Books.

Charlton, Joseph. 2015. "Refugee Crisis: What Life Is Really Like inside the 'Jungle' in Calias." *Independent,* September 30. http://www .independent.co.uk/news/world/europe/refugee-crisis-what-life-is -really-like-inside-the-jungle-in-calais-a6674256.html.

Cone, Devon. 2015. "The Process for Interviewing, Vetting, and Resettling Syrian Refugees in America Is Incredibly Long and Thorough." *Foreign Policy,* November 30. http://foreignpolicy.com/2015/11/30/the -process-for-interviewing-vetting-and-resettling-syrian-refugees-in -america-is-incredibly-long-and-thorough/.

Courbet, David. 2016. "Migrants at Calais Camp Given Dignity in Death." *The Local,* May 23. https://www.thelocal.fr/20160523/migrants-at -calais-camp-given-dignity-in-death.

Derrida, Jacques. 1984. "No Apocalypse, Not Now (Full Speed Ahead, Seven Missiles, Seven Missives)." *Diacritics* 14, no. 2: 20–31.

——. 2001. *On Cosmopolitanism and Forgiveness.* New York: Routledge.

——. 2003. "Hostipitality." *Angelaki: Journal of the Theoretical Humanities* 5, no. 3: 3–18.

——. 2005. *Rogues: Two Essays on Reason.* Stanford, Calif.: Stanford University Press.

——. 2006. *H.C. for Life, That Is to Say . . .* Stanford, Calif.: Stanford University Press.

——. 2008. *The Animal That Therefore I Am.* New York: Fordham University Press.

——. 2009a. *The Beast and the Sovereign, Volume 1.* Chicago: University of Chicago Press.

——. 2009b. "Unconditionality or Sovereignty: The University at the Frontiers of Europe." *Oxford Literary Review* 31, no. 2: 115–31.

——. 2013. *The Death Penalty, Volume 1.* Chicago: University of Chicago Press.

Derrida, Jacques, and Anne Dufourmantelle. 2000. *Of Hospitality.* Stanford, Calif.: Stanford University Press.

Dijkhorst, Hilde van, and Suzette Vonhof. 2005. *Gender and Humanitarian Aid: A Literature Review of Policy and Practice.* Wageningen: Netherlands: Department of Disaster Studies, Wageningen University.

Dobbs, Leo. 2008. "UNHCR Backs 16 Days of Opposition to Violence against Women." United Nations High Commissioner for Refugees. Last modified November 25. http://www.unhcr.org/en-us/news/latest /2008/11/492c1eb74/unhcr-backs-16-days-opposition-violence-against -women.html.

Dobkowski, Michael N., and Isidor Wallimann. 1989. *Radical Perspectives on the Rise of Fascism in Germany.* New York: Monthly Review Press.

Edwards, Adrian. 2016. "Global Force Displacement Hits Record High." United Nations Refugee Agency. Last modified June 20. http:// www.unhcr.org/en-us/news/latest/2016/6/5763b65a4/global-forced -displacement-hits-record-high.html.

European Commission. 2016. "Implementing the EU–Turkey Statement— Questions and Answers." June 15. http://europa.eu/rapid/press-release _MEMO-16-1664_en.htm.

Fassin, Didier. 2016. "From Right to Favor: The Refugee Question as Moral Crisis." *The Nation,* April 5. https://www.thenation.com/article/from -right-to-favor/.

Ferris, Elizabeth G. 2007. "Abuse of Power: Sexual Exploitation of Refugee Women and Girls." *Signs: Journal of Women in Culture and Society* 32, no. 3: 584–91.

Finnerty, Deirdre. 2015. "Migrant Crisis: Trauma Takes Toll on Mental Health." BBC News. Last modified December 22. http://www.bbc.com /news/world-europe-35102320.

Fleming, Melissa. 2015. "Crossings of Mediterranean Sea Exceed 300,000, Including 200,000 to Greece." United Nations Refugee Agency. Last modified August 28. http://www.unhcr.org/en-us/news/latest/2015/8 /55e06a5b6/crossings-mediterranean-sea-exceed-300000-including -200000-greece.html.

Gentleman, Amelia. 2015. "The Horror of the Calais Refugee Camp: 'We Feel Like We Are Dying Slowly.'" *The Guardian,* November 3. https:// www.theguardian.com/world/2015/nov/03/refugees-horror-calais -jungle-refugee-camp-feel-like-dying-slowly.

Golden, Janet. 2016. "What Will Today's Immigration Detention Centers Look Like to Future Americans?" *Philadelphia Inquirer,* June 22. http://www.philly.com/philly/blogs/public_health/What-will-todays -immigration-detention-centers-look-like-to-future-Americans-.html.

Granski, Megan, Allen Keller, and Homer Venters. 2015. "Death Rates among Detained Immigrants in the United States." *International Journal of Environmental Research and Public Health* 12: 14414– 14419.

Greenspan, Jesse. 2013. "7 Red Cross Facts." History. Last modified October 29. http://www.history.com/news/7-things-you-may-not -know-about-the-red-cross.

Haddad, Samir. 2013. *Derrida and the Inheritance of Democracy.* Bloomington: Indiana University Press.

Halley, Janet, and Wendy Brown, eds. 2002. *Left Legalism/Left Critique.* Durham, N.C.: Duke University Press.

Herzog, Johann Jakob, and Philip Schaff. 2011. *The New Schaff–Herzog Encyclopedia of Religious Knowledge.* Charleston: Nabu Press.

Hrala, Josh. 2016. "Global Warming Could Trigger a 'Climate Exodus' from the Middle East and North Africa." Science Alert. Last modified

May 4. http://www.sciencealert.com/global-warming-may-trigger-a
-climate-exodus-in-parts-of-the-middle-east-and-north-africa.

Human Rights First. 2009a. "U.S. Detention of Asylum Seekers: Seeking
Protection, Finding Prison." Last modified April. http://www
.humanrightsfirst.org/wp-content/uploads/pdf/090429-RP-hrf
-asylum-detention-report.pdf.

———. 2009b. "Will the Immigration Detention System Finally Get the
Reforms It Desperately Needs?" Last modified August 7. http://www
.humanrightsfirst.org/2009/08/07/will-the-immigration-detention
-system-finally-get-the-reforms-it-desperately-needs.

Human Rights Watch. 2016. "US: Deaths in Immigration Detention:
Newly Released Records Suggest Dangerous Lapses in Medical Care."
Last modified July 7. https://www.hrw.org/news/2016/07/07/us
-deaths-immigration-detention.

Internal Displacement Monitoring Center. 2015. "19.3 Million Displaced
by Disasters but 'Mother Nature Not to Blame' Says New Report."
Last modified July 20. http://www.internal-displacement.org/assets/
library/Media/201507-globalEstimates-2015/20150706-GE-2015Press
-release-FINAL-v1.pdf.

Kant, Immanuel. 1999. *Religion within the Boundaries of Mere Reason: And
Other Writings*. Cambridge: Cambridge University Press.

———. 2015. *Natural Science*. Cambridge: Cambridge University Press.

Kelley, Colin P., Shahrzad Mohtadib, Mark A. Canec, Richard Seagerc, and
Yochanan Kushnir. 2015. "Climate Change in the Fertile Crescent and
Implications of the Recent Syrian Drought." *Proceedings of the National
Academy of Sciences of the United States of America* 112, no. 11: 3241–46.

Kennedy, Duncan. 2002. "The Critique of Rights in Critical Legal
Studies." In *Left Legalism/Left Critique,* edited by Wendy Brown and
Janet Halley, 178–228. Durham, N.C.: Duke University Press.

Klein, Naomi. 2007. *The Shock Doctrine: The Rise of Disaster Capitalism*.
New York: Picador.

Lawler, Leonard. 2014. "Jacques Derrida." In *The Stanford Encyclopedia of
Philosophy,* edited by Edward N. Zalta. Last modified March 19. http://
plato.stanford.edu/archives/spr2014/entries/derrida/.

Lemkin, Raphael. 2005. *Axis Rule in Occupied Europe: Laws of Occupation,
Analysis of Government, Proposals for Redress*. Clark, N.J.: The
Lawbook Exchange.

Levene, Mark. 2005. *Genocide in the Age of the Nation State*. Vol. 1, *The
Meaning of Genocide*. London: I. B. Tauris.

Liu, Lydia H. 2014. "Shadows of Universalism: The Untold Story of Human
Rights around 1948." *Critical Inquiry* 40: 385–417.

Local. 2016. "Cover-Up Claim over NYE Mass Sexual Assaults." January 4.
http://www.thelocal.de/20160104/refugees-blamed-for-mass-sexual
-assault-in-cologne.

McClelland, Mac. 2014. "How to Build a Perfect Refugee Camp." *New York Times Magazine,* February 13. http://www.nytimes.com/2014/02/16/magazine/how-to-build-a-perfect-refugee-camp.html?_r=0.

McKenzie, David, and Brent Swails. 2015. "Sanctuary without End: The Refugees the World Forgot." CNN. http://www.cnn.com/interactive/2015/10/world/dadaab-refugees/.

Meyers, Diana Tietjens. 2016. *Victims' Stories and the Advancement of Human Rights.* Oxford: Oxford University Press.

Midlarsky, Manus I. 2005. *The Killing Trap: Genocide in the Twentieth Century.* Cambridge: Cambridge University Press.

Miller, Liz. 2011. "The Irony of Refuge: Gender-Based Violence against Female Refugees in Africa." *Human Rights and Human Welfare: Topical Research Digest: Minority Digest,* 77–90.

Momodu, Sulaiman. 2015. "Refugees Turn to Ethiopia for Safety and Asylum: Country Now Hosts the Largest Number of Refugees in Africa." Africa Renewal. Last modified March 30. http://www.un.org/africarenewal/magazine/april-2015/refugees-turn-to-ethiopia-safety-and-asylum.

Naas, Michael. 2009. "Miracle and Machine: Derrida's Faith." *Research in Phenomenology* 39, no. 2: 184–203.

———. 2014. *The End of the World and Other Teachable Moments: Jacques Derrida's Final Seminar.* New York: Fordham University Press.

Nail, Thomas. 2016. "A Tale of Two Crises: Migration and Terrorism after the Paris Attacks." *Studies in Ethnicity and Nationalism* 16, no. 1: 158–67.

Nazario, Sonia. 2015. "The Refugees at Our Door: We Are Paying Mexico to Keep People from Reaching Our Border, People Who Are Fleeing Central American Violence." *New York Times,* October 10. http://www.nytimes.com/2015/10/11/opinion/sunday/the-refugees-at-our-door.html.

Neuman, Michael, and Fabrice Weissman, eds. 2016. *Saving Lives and Staying Alive: The Professionalization of Humanitarian Security.* London: Hurst.

Office of the UN Special Adviser on the Prevention of Genocide. n.d. "Analysis Framework." http://www.un.org/en/preventgenocide/adviser/pdf/osapg_analysis_framework.pdf.

Oliver, Kelly. 2001. *Witnessing: Beyond Recognition.* Minneapolis: University of Minnesota Press.

———. 2007. *Women as Weapons of War: Iraq, Sex and the Media.* New York: Columbia University Press.

———. 2013. *Technologies of Life and Death: From Cloning to Capital Punishment.* New York: Fordham University Press.

———. 2015. *Earth and World.* New York: Columbia University Press.

———. 2016a. "Death as Penalty and the Fantasy of Instant Death." *Journal of Law and Critique* 27, no. 2: 137–49.

———. 2016b. *Hunting Girls: Sexual Violence from "The Hunger Games" to Campus Rape.* New York: Columbia University Press.

———. Forthcoming. "The Special Plight of Refugee Women." In *Decolonizing Feminism: Transnational Feminism and Globalization,* edited by Margaret A. McClaren. London: Rowman and Littlefield International.

Owen, David. 2014. "Human Rights, Refugees and Freedom of Movement." *Journal for Human Rights* 1, no. 2: 50–65.

———. 2016a. "In Loco Civitatis: On the Normative Structure of the International Refugee Regime." In *Migration in Political Theory,* edited by Sarah Fine and Lea Ypi, 269–90. Oxford: Oxford University Press.

———. 2016b. "Refugees, Economic Migrants, and Weak Cosmopolitanism." *Critical Review of International Social and Political Philosophy,* September, 1–10.

———. 2016c. "Refugees, Fairness, and Taking Up the Slack." *Moral Philosophy and Politics* 3, no. 2: 141–64.

Rancière, Jacques. 2004. "Who Is the Subject of the Rights of Man?" *The South Atlantic Quarterly* 103: 297–310.

Refugee Council. 2009. "The Vulnerable Women's Project: Refugee and Asylum Seeking Women Affected by Rape or Sexual Violence." http://www.refugeecouncil.org.uk/assets/0001/7039/RC_VWP-report-web.pdf.

Rosemont, Henry, Jr. 1991. "Rights-Bearing Individual and Role-Bearing Persons." In *Rules, Rituals, and Responsibility: Essays Dedicated to Herbert Fingarette,* edited by Mary I. Bockover, 71–102. La Salle, Ill.: Open Court.

RT News. 2016. "Almost 130 Refugee Kids Vanish after 'Calais Jungle' Demolition—Charity." April 3. https://www.rt.com/news/338217-129-kids-missing-in-calais/.

Schwartzstein, Peter. 2016. "The Climate-Change Refugee Crisis Is Only Just Beginning." *Quartz* (blog), January 31. http://qz.com/605609/the-climate-change-refugee-crisis-is-only-just-beginning/.

Shams, Alex. 2016. "Neither Taharrush Gamea nor Sexism Are Arab 'Cultural Practices.'" *Huffington Post,* January 21. http://www.huffingtonpost.com/alex-shams/sexism-isnt-an-arab-cultural-practice_b_9022056.html.

Shaw, Martin. 2015. *What Is Genocide?* London: Polity.

Spencer, Richard. 2016. "Nearly Half a Million Pregnant Women among Displaced and Refugee Syrians." *The Telegraph,* February 3. http://www.telegraph.co.uk/news/worldnews/middleeast/syria/12139358/Nearly-half-a-million-pregnant-women-among-displaced-and-refugee-Syrians.html.

Sputnik International. 2016. "A Closer Look at 'Europe's Worst' Refugee Camp." Last modified January 24. https://sputniknews.com/europe/20160124/1033644952/dunkirk-france-refugee-camp.html.

Tazzioli, Martina. 2015. "The Politics of Counting and the Scene of Rescue: Border Deaths in the Mediterranean." *Radical Philosophy: Philosophy Journal of the Independent Left,* July/August, 1–6.

———. 2016. "Border Displacements: Challenging the Politics of Rescue between Mare Nostrum and Triton." *Migration Studies* 4, no. 1: 1–19.

Thompson, John L., and Gail A. Quets. 1987. *Redefining the Moral Order: Towards a Normative Theory of Genocide.* New York: Columbia University Press.

Timár, Andrea. 2015. "Derrida and the Immune System." *Et al.—Critical Theory Online* 3. http://etal.hu/en/archive/terrorism-and-aesthetics -2015/derrida-and-the-immune-system/.

Timár, Eszter. 2014. "Squirm." *Inter/Alia: Bodily Fluids* 9: 35–48.

———. 2016. "Autoreactivity and Immunotolerance: A Derridean Immunology." Paper presented at the fifth Derrida Today Conference, Goldsmiths, University of London, June 8–11.

United Nations. 2014. "Framework of Analysis for Atrocity Crimes: A Tool for Prevention." http://www.un.org/en/preventgenocide/adviser/pdf/ framework%20of%20analysis%20for%20atrocity%20crimes_en.pdf.

United Nations General Assembly. 1951. *Convention Relating to the Status of Refugees.* July 28. http://www.refworld.org/docid/3be01b964.html.

United Nations High Commissioner for Refugees. 1995a. "Human Rights and Refugee Protection (RLD 5)." http://www.unhcr.org/publ/PUBL /3ae6bd900.pdf.

———. 1995b. "Interviewing Applicants for Refugee Status (RLD 4)." http:// www.unhcr.org/4d9485a69.pdf.

———. 2015a. *Global Trends 2015.* http://www.unhcr.org/en-us/figures-at-a -glance.html.

———. 2015b. "Women on the Run." Last modified October. http://www .unhcr.org/en-us/publications/operations/5630f24c6/women-run .html.

———. n.d. "Safe Motherhood in Refugee Camps." http://www.unhcr.org /456c56ea2.pdf.

United Nations Population Fund for Arab States. 2016. "Women and Girls in the Syria Crisis: UNFPA Response." https://www.unfpa.org/sites/ default/files/resource-pdf/UNFPA-FACTSANDFIGURES-5%5B4%5D .pdf.

Weiss, Thomas G. 2013. *Humanitarian Business.* London: Polity.

Weizman, Eyal. 2007. *Hollow Land: Israel's Architecture of Occupation.* London: Verso.

———. 2011. *The Least of All Possible Evils: Humanitarian Violence from Arendt to Gaza.* London: Verso.

Wendle, John. 2015. "The Ominous Story of Syria's Climate Refugees: Farmers Who Have Escaped the Battle-Torn Nation Explain How Drought and Government Abuse Have Driven Social Violence."

Scientific American, December 17. http://www.scientificamerican.com/article/ominous-story-of-syria-climate-refugees/.

Wessel, Julia Schulze. 2015. "On Border Subjects: Rethinking the Figure of the Refugee and the Undocumented Migrant." *Constellations* 23, no. 1: 46–57.

Wills, David. 2014. "Drone Penalty." *SubStance* 43, no. 2: 174–92.

Worley, Will, and Lizzie Dearden. 2016. "Greek Refugee Camp Is 'as Bad as a Nazi Concentration Camp,' Says Minister." *The Independent,* March 18. http://www.independent.co.uk/news/world/europe/idomeni-refugee-dachau-nazi-concentration-camp-greek-minister -a6938826.html.

Yardley, Jim, and Gaia Pianigiani. 2016. "Three Days, 700 Deaths on Mediterranean as Migrant Crisis Flares." *New York Times,* May 29, A1, A6.

Kelly Oliver is W. Alton Jones Professor of Philosophy at Vanderbilt University. She is the author of more than one hundred articles, thirteen books, and ten edited volumes, including, most recently, *Hunting Girls: Sexual Violence from "The Hunger Games" to Campus Rape* and *Earth and World: Philosophy after the Apollo Missions*. She has also written three Jessica James, Cowgirl Philosopher mysteries.